RICHARD G. COX LIBR.
UN. OF SOUTHERN MISS. - GULF PARK

The
Research Universities
and Their Patrons

ADVISORY COMMITTEE

THOMAS A. BARTLETT president, Association of American Universities
WILLARD L. BOYD president, University of Iowa
WILLIAM G. BOWEN president, Princeton University
WILLIAM H. DANFORTH chancellor, Washington University
SHELDON HACKNEY president, University of Pennsylvania
ARTHUR G. HANSEN president, Purdue University
STEVEN MULLER president, Johns Hopkins University
JAMES C. OLSON president, University of Missouri
DAVID S. SAXON president, University of California System
ROBERT H. STROTZ president, Northwestern University
CHARLES E. YOUNG chancellor, University of California, Los Angeles
JAMES I. ARMSTRONG president, Charles A. Dana Foundation
RICHARD LYMAN president, Rockefeller Foundation
ROBERT L. PAYTON president, Exxon Education Foundation
ALAN PIFER president, Carnegie Corporation of New York
ALBERT REES president, Alfred P. Sloan Foundation
JOHN E. SAWYER president, Andrew W. Mellon Foundation
FRANKLIN THOMAS president, Ford Foundation
EDWARD DONLEY chairman, Air Products and Chemicals
GERALD D. LAUBACH president, Pfizer, Incorporated
WILLIAM F. MILLER president, SRI International
MORRIS TANENBAUM executive vice-president, AT&T

The
Research
Universities
and Their Patrons

ROBERT M. ROSENZWEIG
with
Barbara Turlington

Prepared under the auspices of the
Association of American Universities

University of California Press
Berkeley ▪ Los Angeles ▪ London

RICHARD G. COX LIBRARY
UN. OF SOUTHERN MISS. - GULF PARK

University of California Press
Berkeley and Los Angeles, California
University of California Press, Ltd.
London, England

© 1982 by
The Regents of the University of California

Library of Congress Cataloging in Publication Data
Rosenzweig, Robert M.
  The research universities and their patrons.

  Includes index.
    1. Research institutes—United States.   2. Federal
aid to research—United States. 3. Science and state—
United States. I. Turlington, Barbara. II. Title.
Q180.U5R67   001.4'0973   81-19685
ISBN 0-520-04664-1   AACR2

Printed in the United States of America
1   2   3   4   5   6   7   8   9

CONTENTS

FOREWORD

In the thirty-five years since the Second World War, the United States has created a unique national system for conducting basic research and advanced training. The system is a complex set of connections between research universities and federal agencies that support research. It is a pragmatic system, constantly evolving and needing reinterpretation to the many publics it serves.

The system has grown and developed because it has proved to be productive, efficient, and powerful. Research and advanced training go together, and the university provides for them an admirable institutional setting. However, the pragmatic and complicated character of the enterprise poses some special problems.

Research universities are extraordinarily diverse in what transpires within their confines. They are general teaching institutions and have their greatest public recognition in that context. They provide public services of every kind, from extension work in agriculture to entertainment on Saturday afternoons. They also carry on research and training that set the world standard.

Of the major activities in a research university, the research component has the most uncertain forms of financial support. Many people take for granted that basic research and advanced training will be done in our research universities and assume that these will somehow be financed, largely under diverse federal programs. With changing federal priorities and federal programs, however, the nation must either reaffirm its traditional modes of support for basic research (the National Science Foundation, the National Institutes of Health, programs in the Department of Defense, the Department of Energy, the Department of Agriculture, etc.) or must establish additional forms, perhaps through tax incentives for industry. If we do neither, we shall see the United States' leadership in basic research, with all that means, passing to other nations.

This study, prepared at the instigation of the Association of American Universities, identifies steps necessary to maintain or restore university capacity for advanced training and research. Its recommendations aim at reinforcing the vitality and productiveness of research universities. On behalf of the Association of American Universities, I am deeply grateful to the authors for their insights and eloquence and to those foundation, industrial and university leaders who assisted with comments and criticism. These papers deserve to be read; their recommendations confront us with choices we may accept or reject but cannot ignore if we expect to maintain world leadership in the search for knowledge.

Thomas A. Bartlett
President, Association of American Universities
Washington, D.C.

PREFACE

This is the second report in five years on the condition and needs of the nation's major research universities. The first, published in December 1977 under the title *Research Universities and the National Interest*, described its purpose as follows:

> The relations between the needs of the nation and the responsibilities of organized education are massive and complex. The report we present here is the result of an effort by one group of educators to address a relatively small but crucial part of those relations: the places where the national interest and the consequent responsibilities of the federal government intersect with the special capabilities of the nation's research universities.

The five years that have passed since the preparation of that document have been, by any standard, eventful years for universities, for government, and for the nation that is served by both. It is time to take another look, to see what has happened to the major universities, to reassess their relations with the national government, to look at specific issues and the responsibility for them, and to provide an agenda of action for the period ahead.

Even if there were no other reasons, the accession to office of a new national administration committed to a different philosophy of government from its predecessors would be reason enough to take a new look, a look back to establish continuities of policy and a look ahead to chart future directions. The first year of the Reagan administration provided mixed signals about its long-run intentions with respect to higher education generally and research universities in particular. On the positive side, even in a year marked by deep cuts in domestic social programs, most research budgets were relatively well protected. More troublesome was the thoroughgoing effort to reduce appropriations for social science research and the proposed, though happily not successful, elimination of the National Science Foundation's Graduate Fellowship Program.

The first Reagan budget was put together hastily, and its main driving force was the determination to reduce domestic expenditures. Only time will tell whether it was also founded in an informed and coherent view of what is required by way of policy in order to assure the continuation of the high quality research for which the budget reflected such a high regard. There is no better time than now to try to describe the links between the research product and the facilities, equipment, libraries, and people without which there will be in the end no product worth having.

Neither the earlier report nor this one purports to cover the whole of a group of institutions so rich and complex as the research universities. Undergraduate education, professional education, and continuing education are major components of some or all of these institutions, but they are not addressed here as central topics. Rather, our focus is on the status and prospects of that set of activities that distinguishes these universities from all others: research and the training for research. Even within that narrower compass, more attention is directed to some topics than to others. There is more here about science and technology than about the humanities and the performing arts. This emphasis is dictated by the history of public policy, not by any sense that science is more central to the nature or purposes of these institutions than are other fields. This report, like the first one, speaks to the humanities and social sciences through its concern for the condition of research libraries and programs of international and foreign area studies. They, too, are only partial expressions of the humanistic and social scientific range of the university. Perhaps the truth is that there is no way of comprehending the whole of the research university's scope in a single effort. Recognition of that truth is the best antidote to distortion.

In one important respect, the organizing premise of this report differs from that of the first. The earlier report spoke almost exclusively to government, to its responsibilities for the research universities and to ways of effectuating those responsibilities. The report constituted open recognition that government had become a major actor in the life of these institutions and a plea that its policies ought to add up to a thoughtful and consistent approach to them. The present work accepts the premise of the first report as a given and in addition argues that the research universities must assess realistically the government's capabilities and limitations and must assume the responsibility to define their own needs in light of that assessment. This will mean finding policies that minimize, to the extent possible, institutional dependency on long-term governmental commitments while still assuring the needed resources for important activities. It will mean seeking new alliances and new patterns of mutual interest so that the inevitable ups and downs of politics can be buffered by the workings of multiple relationships.

A few comments on the chapters that follow may help to explain why this, rather than some other set of issues, was chosen. The topics of graduate training, international and foreign area studies, and research libraries were also dealt with in *Research Universities and the National Interest*. They are examined again here because they remain important elements of the research universities and because they continue to present significant, unresolved issues of policy. An entire chapter is devoted here to the growing deficiencies in research instrumentation and facilities. That it is necessary to have such a chapter is testimony to the way in which slow deterioration, if unmonitored, can accumulate until it is suddenly recognized as a crisis. This chapter can stand as a metaphor for the effects on all of higher education of a decade of tight finances. It is unusual for institutions to die; it is far more common for them to grow slowly less good.

The chapter on the universities and business has no antecedent in the earlier report. That is a sign of how rapidly events change perceptions. Sustained problems of low productivity and intense foreign competition have rekindled business interest in universities as sources of innovation, and an increasingly changeable federal government has moved universities toward business as a source of funds and as a buffer against government. In addition to the separate chapter on the subject, each of the other chapters addresses ways in which closer interaction between business and universities would be advantageous to both.

Culture and the institutions that sustain it have always depended on enlightened patronage. That is as true for the modern, sophisticated research university as it was for Michelangelo and Mozart. It is a somewhat more recent truth, however, one born out of the rise of modern organizations, that their fate lies largely in the hands of those who work in them. In the most profound sense, the well-being of the research universities rests on decisions made by their faculties, administrations, and trustees. No patrons, however enlightened they might be, should be asked to do more than to sustain the values that are articulated by those charged with the primary responsibility. Difficult decisions lie ahead as patterns of support change, as new pressures are added onto old ones, and as new alliances present value conflicts that test again the central purposes of universities. That the process of testing continues is a sign of health, an indication that universities retain an important place in the life of a vibrant society. For that condition to continue will require enlightened and generous patrons working with faculties and administrations who know what they are about and why.

The papers that comprise this report were commissioned by the Association of American Universities. The principal author and his associate were given the gift of time with which to think and write by the generosity of the following foundations:

Carnegie Corporation of New York
Charles A. Dana Foundation
Exxon Education Foundation
Ford Foundation
Andrew W. Mellon Foundation
Rockefeller Foundation
Alfred P. Sloan Foundation

The project has been guided by an advisory committee consisting of university presidents, foundation officers, and business executives. Their involvement has been active and thoughtful; the importance that they attached to the task was shown time and again by their dedication to insightful criticism.

The arguments and conclusions of this report are different from what they would have been without the participation of these advisors. Still, it is important to emphasize, first, that they acted as individuals and not as spokesmen of their organizations and, second, that their general agreement to the lines of argument and conclusions found here do not signify unanimity on all the issues. As a group, they stand as one in their commitment to the research university; on broad lines of policy, they are nearly one; on matters of emphasis or particular points of analysis, there was considerable diversity. We hope for the same kinds of responses from our readers.

CHAPTER ONE

THE CLIMATE OF POLICYMAKING

BACKGROUND

A research university is one whose mores and practices make it clear that enlarging and disseminating knowledge are equally important activities and that each is done better when both are done in the same place by the same people. The United States can boast of institutions that do distinguished teaching as their main activity and of others that devote their full efforts to high-quality research, but what sets the American university scene apart from all others is the existence of this group of institutions whose commitment is both to teaching and to research and to the belief that the interaction of the two brings added value to both.

Is the belief more than that? Is it more than simply a conviction born of convenience and of the ease of justifying existing structures? Evidence for the value of particular forms of social organization is notoriously difficult to find. In the real world, genuine comparisons—the kind that support confident generalizations—rarely exist. Notwithstanding such limitations, most informed observers throughout the world would agree that the American research university must be judged a success by virtually any imaginable standard of measurement. It has been the home to research and scholarship that, across all fields and in the aggregate, are unexcelled anywhere in the world; it has trained research scientists and scholars of the highest quality, as well as doctors, lawyers, and managers of great sophistication; it has, notwithstanding a commitment to basic research, retained a connection to the worlds of commerce and affairs that enriches commercial and public life in great measure. To maintain a watchful concern for the health of these relatively few institutions does not require blindness to their faults or unrelieved admiration for all of their works, only a sense of how extraordinary it is to have a set of institutions whose net social value is so great and how difficult it is to repair serious damage to them.

The existence of these universities, perhaps fifty to seventy-five in all, represents a remarkable achievement. A form of social organization barely known elsewhere in the world has so clearly demonstrated its value in the United States that the wisdom of sustaining it is almost beyond serious debate. Although it may now seem so, it is important to recall that this result was not inevitable. Much of the scientific work that proved the practical value of science during World War II was done by university scientists, but not in truly academic settings. There was no necessary reason to conclude from that experience that both research and teaching would be better if they were done together. The tradition of the research university was not widespread or well entrenched in this country. On the contrary, the main existing examples of how to conduct basic research were those from institutions in Great Britain and the Continent and from the experiences of the war; to emulate these could well have led to a different conclusion. That those examples did not become America's model is a significant achievement of both education and politics.

In the years that followed the war, the competition of the cold war maintained high public interest in science and technology as the foundation of military preparedness, and it also provided the momentum for initiatives as diverse as the space program and the stimulation of programs of research and teaching in foreign languages and cultures. The effect was to confirm the value of the university to important national purposes.

In addition to the Cold War, other forces moved in the same direction. The arrival of relative peace and unquestioned prosperity helped to move the national concern for health to a high place on the list of social and political priorities. The cure of disease was seen early to depend on knowledge of basic biological processes, and as a consequence, the National Institutes of Health became the instrument for the expansion of health-related research and training in university laboratories. Similarly, the extension of social insurance programs to health care through Medicare and Medicaid greatly stimulated the need for physicians and other health care personnel and placed the government in the position of major purchaser of health care services, which many university teaching hospitals used as the basis of their training. Thus, from basic research on the structure of life, to the application of research in therapy, to the training of researchers and practitioners, to the delivery of medical service, the university became the instrument of choice by means of an unbreakable mutually dependent relationship with the government.

Other societies addressed similar stimuli with different organizational forms—with academies, institutes, and centers separate from their universities. In the United States, however, the university became the distinctive and central institution for grappling with these and other issues. We chose to combine basic research, a fair mixture of applied research, training for research, and undergraduate education in the same place, done by the same people, frequently at the same time. For all of the problems that arise from such a volatile mixture, the evidence from elsewhere in the world provides no basis for regret at the direction taken here.

To recognize the development and confirmation of the research university as an achievement—a successful product of social choice, educational initiative, and political skill—may help lend perspective to a number of collateral questions. Such issues as the pressures for wider geographical distribution of research funds, the role of peer review in decisions about funding, and the baneful effects of effort reporting requirements, for example, are important; and if they are not dealt with intelligently, they can have a cumulatively corrosive effect on the quality of research and teaching. Fortunately, they arise in the context of a broad intellectual and political consensus over the value of the institutions they affect.

There are other parts of the context from which policy emerges that are not so salubrious. Public policy flows from a climate of events and attitudes that establishes what is necessary and determines what is possible. Thus, some important aspects of the American climate need to be accounted for if sensible policies for the 1980s are to emerge. The main facts of contemporary American life from the perspective of research universities are the corrosive effects of a widespread indifference—even hostility—to the well-being of important social institutions; the equally corrosive effects of rapid and sustained inflation; the active role of government in regulating economic and social activity; and the growing importance of and ambivalence toward science and technology. Even that list is by no means complete, but it suggests a world of sufficient complexity to challenge even the most intrepid among us.

THE PROBLEMS OF INSTITUTIONS

These have not been easy times for the central institutions of American society. The worst of the late 1960s and early 1970s is perhaps behind us, but the legacy of Vietnam and Watergate remains. Instead of the virulent animosity of that period, one senses today at best a widespread skepticism about the capacity of our social institutions, governmental and private alike, to do what is required of them.

There may be some comfort to be taken from the consistent showing in the polls that the public at large retains an ability to discriminate among the objects of its disaffection. In general, institutions of government, business, and the organized professions—what might generally be called the institutions of power and privilege—rank low in public esteem. In contrast, public regard for science, universities, and religious institutions has rebounded from its lowest point.

Unhappily, however, the leaders of opinion seem to be less discriminating. The media delight in exposing the warts of government, education, the judiciary, and anything else in their line of vision. Government too often acts as though its preoccupations of the moment override all other considerations, including the ability of other institutions to perform their roles. Single-interest groups, notoriously unconcerned about anything outside the narrow scope of their particular visions, attack government, business, universities, and the media with ready and equal abandon.

None of this, perhaps, should be surprising. For almost two decades we have been a nation buffeted by shocks and bewildered by a confusion of seemingly intractable problems. We are also a people who like solutions and who have a low tolerance for ambiguity, complexity, and uncertainty. Faced with pressing problems, we press for quick answers. We applaud those who offer them and scorn those who can tell us only how complicated it all is. It is a climate tailor-made for antiinstitutionalism, for institutions are nothing if they are not conservative; it is in their very nature to exalt process over substance, to insist on the importance of continuity and precedent, and to avoid actions that may threaten their survival.

These are extremely valuable qualities; they are, in fact, part of the glue that holds stable societies together over time. It happens, though, that they are out of joint with this particular time. The core of the problem is not the reaction to the well-publicized instances of misfeasance and malfeasance on the part of some; rather, it is that the most valuable and most responsible of our institutions are conveying the least welcome message, namely, that there are no easy solutions, that we must learn to live with our afflictions, and that it is precisely in such circumstances that stability and continuity are of greatest value.

The best universities in the land, those with the intellectually most active faculties and the most able students, are in a particularly difficult bind. They are at one and the same time the most conservative and the most radical of social institutions. They retain their eminence by the most rigorous insistence on high standards of performance and evaluation and by a sometimes painful adherence to the procedures of judgment and of inquiry that have been tested in centuries of experience. It may be paradoxical but it is nevertheless a key truth that by insisting on conservative processes, the best universities guarantee the most radical results.

The examples are legion and they involve every aspect of life. In the sciences, dramatically altered conceptions of the nature of matter in the universe and of the fundamental biological and chemical structures of life—conceptions that demand the sacrifice of old certainties as the price of new understanding—have stemmed primarily from work done by university-based scientists in university laboratories. In the social sciences, work done in a few major universities showed the power of scientific public opinion sampling as a tool for explaining political behavior, a development with profound consequences for the way in which politics is now conducted in this country. In the professions, much of the change in medical practice of the last three decades—improved therapies, new technologies, increasing specialization—can be traced to the work of university-based biomedical sciences. And law school faculty members have been instrumental in generating the justification for new law in such key areas as civil rights, civil liberties, capital punishment, consumer protection, environmental protection, political reform, and a host of others.

All of these are signs of vitality, evidence that universities are in fact the setting for work of profound importance. But it also needs to be said that intellectual labor that has real consequences for the way society does its business is certain to generate controversy. Indeed, the more rapid the rate of change, the more intense will be the anxiety it evokes about the institutions that appear to be responsible for it.

This is not simply an abstract and nameless fear; it is a real problem. One vivid recent example of the institutional risk inherent in producing rapid social change is the continuing debate over physician supply and demand. The conventional wisdom of only a decade ago held that too few doctors were being trained to serve the nation's medical needs. It became high priority public policy to double the number of M.D.'s trained each year by funding the expansion of medical school capacity. The support came in the form of capitation funding—a fixed amount of money per student, with eligibility based on the willingness to expand enrollment. In fact, it worked. About twice as many doctors now enter practice each year, and all the apparatus is in place in the medical schools—faculty, laboratories, clinical opportunities, and so forth—to continue to train doctors at that rate.

But the conventional wisdom has changed, for it appears that simply increasing the number of doctors in practice does not bring medical care to those who are most lacking it. On the contrary, it appears that the effect is to increase the concentration of doctors in those areas that already have the most, to increase medical specialization, and to increase medical cost. The solution seemed clear to two successive national administrations: stop subsidizing the institutions that train doctors. Hence, the sustained and successful attack on capitation funding, the very instrument by which government encouraged increases in M.D. enrollment.

Virtually every aspect of that policy debate has had its origins in universities. The data and analysis that "proved" the doctor shortage and the need for expansion were developed largely in universities, as were much of the data and analysis that "proved" the doctor surplus. The universities were, of course, where doctors were trained, and the movement of doctors toward specialized practice was made possible by the basic and clinical research which took place primarily in universities and by the specialty training programs for which university faculty and staff physicians were also primarily responsible. Yet in all of this decade of debate over a critical issue of public policy, it is hard to find indications of serious concern about the stresses imposed on an institution by such sudden changes of direction. On the contrary, the very institutions that were the successful instrument of the old orthodoxy are now the enemies of the new as they become perceived as nothing more than barriers to reform and special pleaders for outmoded and wasteful subsidies.

Other examples come readily to mind. The sharp curtailment of governmental programs in support of graduate training may be argued on its merits in relation to the market for trained manpower. But there can be no argument that public policy that was informed by an enlightened concern for the present and future welfare of the institutions that must be counted on to meet all of society's needs for highly trained manpower would have proceeded with far more thought and deliberation than in fact it did.

If policymakers and those who influence them are strongly moved to seek short-term effects, then those who are responsible for institutions whose lives and usefulness must extend into the long term have an added burden on them. It is the burden of arguing for an unpopular position. If the debate over policy is to account for institutional considerations, then those who understand institutions must make the case for them. Changing the climate will be difficult but essential if sound policies are to prevail.

INFLATION, RETIREMENT, AND
GOVERNMENT POLICY

A second main element in the institutional climate is the persistence of high rates of inflation. The financial effects of inflation on institutions with limited price flexibility, high labor costs, and a heavy dependence on the generosity of others who are themselves suffering the effects of inflation have been described elsewhere. The social costs of inflation as they affect universities are equally real but perhaps less obvious. As in society at large, sustained inflation in universities has the effect of widening and making more bitter internal cleavages that in ordinary times are bridgeable. Many examples could illustrate the point, but one is especially poignant, both in its human dimensions and in its implications for institutional vitality.

Even in the best of times and places, the relations between senior and junior faculty colleagues have been an odd and complex mixture that frequently includes warmth, collegiality, envy, anxiety, respect, and condescension in some workable combination. This is not the best of times, and the combination is becoming less workable. The most visible sign is the controversy over the national movement to abolish mandatory retirement at a fixed age.

It is an excruciatingly difficult issue for universities to deal with, for it pits the needs of valued senior faculty against the ambitions of younger colleagues and against the need of the institution to assure a steady flow of new talent into the ranks of the faculty. So long as retirement income for senior faculty was seen to be stable and sufficient, retirement could be handled in a humane and decent manner. And so long as faculty size was growing, the need for newcomers could be accommodated. Neither condition now obtains. In most universities, faculty size is fixed for the foreseeable future as enrollments level off or decline along with funds for research. And senior faculty approaching retirement now face the inflation-induced prospect of wholly inadequate pension income. Small wonder that resistance to forced retirement grows.

The institutional stakes are high. The hope for successful recruitment and retention of young minority and women faculty rests in significant measure on not deferring the retirement of present faculty to the point of discouraging the young from entering the profession or preventing those who do from finding jobs. That is a special, and especially difficult, variation of the "young investigator problem" discussed in a later chapter on advanced graduate training. Thus, almost without exception, university presidents have urged the Congress and state legislatures to exempt tenured faculty from laws that prohibit or raise the age of mandatory retirement. They can hardly do otherwise if they are to remain faithful to their responsibility for the future well-being of their institutions. But the effect of their stance is to pit them against the interests of their most senior, loyal, and valued faculty. It is an unhappy and demoralizing circumstance for all parties and one that is certain to worsen the longer we suffer from high rates of inflation.

ATTITUDES TOWARD SCIENCE AND TECHNOLOGY

The postwar growth of the research university has been so closely linked to the growth in importance of science and technology that its future will inevitably be affected by changes in public attitudes about and policies toward those twin engines of modern life.

Universities, and quite distinguished ones, existed in the United States before knowledge began to explode in the physical and biological sciences and in engineering. The idea of the graduate university, imported from Germany, came to America with the founding of the Johns Hopkins University in 1876. Humanistic scholarship flourished long before science came to be done by teams of people in large buildings using equipment whose cost in some cases would have paid for the creation of several of these prewar universities.

This is not the place to examine all of the difficulties encountered in the process of building onto existing institutions, with their own particular traditions, programs of scientific research and training as large as those that now mark the research university. Faculties and administrations have for three decades struggled with the difficulties of sustaining the humanities, accommodating new social sciences and new approaches to old ones, and maintaining balance and morale in a setting in which the resources for growth have been heavily skewed toward limited sectors of the institution.

Those are not signs of ill health. On the contrary, in a living and responsive institution growth is never likely to be balanced or even predictable, and so accommodations to imbalance and unpredictability are a natural part of institutional life. There is a new element in the mix now, a new part of the social climate that may yet have profound consequences but whose effects are wholly unpredictable. The fact is that there are manifest signs of growing public, and hence political, ambivalence to the further growth of science and technology. The environmental movement and the anti–nuclear power movement are organized evidence of that ambivalence. The sharp reaction to the discovery of ways to recombine DNA into new organisms was an early sign of what is quite likely to be a growing debate over genetic manipulation.

What one sees so far are indications, not major effects. It might be that in the end, public turmoil over the pace and uses of scientific and technological innovation will strengthen universities by engaging humanists and social scientists in genuine intellectual collaboration with their scientific and technological colleagues. Signs of that development can be seen already. What may be sensed, then, is not yet a shift in the weather but the hint of a storm off shore. It too is a part of the climate in which policy will be set.

GOVERNMENT AS REGULATOR

Another important element of the social climate is not new, but the full recognition of its dimensions and effects is new to universities. It is the extent to which the conduct of institutions has become subject to the regulatory power of government. The United States is by no means alone in this regard. Indeed, if anything, most other democratic nations of the West started earlier and have gone further in their efforts to use government to guide economic activity, cushion the harsher effects of economic competition, redistribute income, and promote the public's health and safety.

Initially, the power of government was used in this country to stimulate competition by preventing monopoly and to protect against the abuse of power by sectors of industry—for example, transportation and utilities—whose scale was inevitably large and whose power was therefore great. Add to those a relatively small number of governmental activities aimed at protecting public health, and it is not hard to see why universities were relatively untouched by regulatory activities.

By the 1960s, the end of innocence was in sight, and by the 1970s it was truly gone. Three developments coincided to alter circumstances dramatically and irrevocably. The first was simply that universities became too large, important, and visible to ignore any longer. The maintenance worker in the university could not be denied the protection of the government for his right to join a union on the grounds that universities were not really engaged in commerce or were somehow too small or idiosyncratic to be reached by the same law that protected the rights of maintenance workers across the street.

Second, the very nature of regulation changed in ways that made universities central rather than peripheral to the regulatory purpose. When, for example, government assumed the duty to redress the effects of two centuries of racial discrimination, it was inconceivable that schools at any level could be exempt. Similarly, the dramatic shift of public focus from the regulation of certain kinds of economic activity to the use of regulatory powers to protect against risks and hazards of many kinds brought universities into the regulatory arena more fully than before. Environmental protection, consumer protection, protection of the subjects of research, protection against toxic wastes—all of those at a minimum include and in some cases focus on universities as sources of hazard from which the public arguably needs protection.

The perception, therefore, that government reaches more broadly and deeply into university activities than ever before is quite accurate. However, the belief of some that universities are uniquely put upon in this respect would be largely incorrect were it not for the third and most recent of the regulatory impulses, the one that has come under the heading of "accountability."

The principle of accountability—in simplest terms, the requirement that recipients of public funds be able to demonstrate that they used the money for the purposes for which it was given—is hardly controversial. Controversy, and it is bitter indeed, arises over the insistence by government on forms of documentation that are widely believed in academic circles to be unreasonable, intrusive, burdensome, and useless, to use only terms that imply no malevolent motives.

At present, the controversy over accountability centers on the requirements for the documentation of faculty effort to support government payments for the direct and indirect costs of research. It is no exaggeration to describe the dispute as virulent. Many faculty bitterly resent having to account for the division of their time into such categories as research, teaching, and administration, activities which often take place simultaneously and which are therefore indistinguishable from one another. The accumulation of data that angers and demeans the giver and is of no practical use to the receiver is at best a dubious activity. It is also a wholly unnecessary controversy. The careful and balanced report of the National Commission on Research[1] proposes several ways to assure accountability by institutions without the burdensome and contentious requirements that now obtain. The willingness of the current administration to consider alternative ways to achieve the same end is encouraging.

The failure to reach an acceptable accommodation on the proper scope and method of accounting for the use of faculty effort would have effects larger than the intrinsic importance of the issue itself. The bitterness generated by rules that are widely believed in academic circles to be unnecessary and insulting is a serious diversion from the im-

---

[1] National Commission on Research, *Accountability: Restoring the Quality of the Partnership* (Washington, D.C., 1980).

portant work of science and government, and also concentration on this issue inhibits a full understanding of the sources and effects of regulation as a whole.

It is tempting, because it is easy, to think of regulation as the product of careless legislators or overreaching bureaucrats or, alternatively, as the product of liberals on social issues and conservatives on financial issues. There is perhaps some truth to each of those, but they are all wide of the mark. The tide of deregulation in recent years has helped to roll back certain restraints on airlines and truckers, and others may follow. It has also helped to call attention to excesses in other areas. It is unlikely, however, that today's reaction will reverse the conditions of modern life that lead citizens to call on government for protection from the hazards that modern life produces or the economic conditions that lead to tight controls on the use of public funds or to the drive to remedy the legacy of racial, ethnic, and sexual discrimination.

The persistence of conditions that lead government to control the conduct of other institutions whose activities affect the public may seem to present a discouraging prospect. But it also suggests a strategy that assumes that issues of government regulation will be with us for the foreseeable future, that they are in fact a continuing part of the social climate, and that no single conflict can be treated as though it will be the last one, if only it can be won. The responsibility of political leaders is to define areas in which protection of the public's interest can be achieved only by regulatory activity; the responsibility of those in universities is to define the areas in which the intrusion of government so distorts institutional purposes and processes that the regulatory end being sought must defer to the damage that regulation will cause.

The action of the government in 1976 to use continued eligibility for medical school capitation funds as a lever to control admission to medical schools in order to achieve what then seemed a pressing purpose—namely, to bring back to American medical schools American nationals who were studying medicine abroad—is an instructive

case. Some in government learned that there is a cost to abuse of the influence that derives from the appropriation of money; some in universities learned that vigorous and timely action can in fact roll back unacceptable acts of government; and in the field of the financing of medical education, at least, much was learned about the forms of support that are most likely to produce the temptation to government to overreach its proper influence and that make institutional dependence highest and the possibility of resistance lowest.

The issues here are both important and timely. An early move by President Reagan to establish a task force on regulation under the leadership of Vice President Bush has opened the prospect of redressing some regulatory excesses. Institutions of higher education, represented by the American Council on Education, responded promptly with an agenda of reforms. It is too early to know what may result, but it is fair to say that the accomplishments in this area of an administration that is philosophically committed to deregulation probably will be the maximum that can be achieved in a move back from the present condition. That fact is also known to those groups that are committed to preserving the protections of government. Therefore, the decisions made in the next year or two will be uncommonly important and hotly contested.

Persistence, intelligence, and restraint are such frequently advised strategies that they may seem to be no strategies at all. In protracted struggles with high stakes, however, they constitute the only workable strategy available.

GOVERNMENT AS PATRON

Finally, in this assessment of the policymaking climate, it is necessary to look at the role of government as the main stimulus of the postwar development of the research university and as the continuing largest single patron of research and research training.

In approaching this very large and important topic, one must note that it is now a part of the American policy consensus that the federal government bears an important share of the responsibility for sustaining a vital research base at the research universities. To put the matter in this way purposely begs the very important questions of the size of the share and the best means for supplying it. However, those are the stuff of policy, and policy rests on the fundamental points of consensus: that there exists a federal responsibility and that it is shared with others. Both of these points need to be examined, for the failure to think clearly about them has contributed to some current difficulties.

Historically, the responsibility for the material support of U.S. universities has been assumed by state governments in the public sector and by private philanthropy and student fees in the private. The federal government played a significant but small role, chiefly by means of land grants and by a few modest programs of financial grants. Until almost the middle of this century there was nothing that could be described as a serious federal commitment to the continuing support of higher education. It is not coincidental that until the middle of this century there were no more than a handful of institutions in which the responsibility of the faculty to engage in original research was taken seriously. A major exception to that generalization is the field of agricultural research, to which the national government and a defined set of institutions created by it had strong commitments.

We now live in a different world, and while it is merely melodrama to argue, as some do, that the major American universities have become in some sense "federal universities," wards and helpless dependents of the government, it is surely true that the enormous growth of government programs has produced large and lasting changes in the shape and style of institutional life. In 1940, total funds available for scientific research in universities from all sources were $31 million. In fiscal year 1979, the National Science Foundation alone spent about twenty-five times that amount in its programs of research support while total government support for university-based research surpassed $3 billion. The sheer magnitude of the enterprise had its own effects on institutions, but the dominance of a single patron was itself a fact of significance. That single patron was so openhanded, so generally enlightened, and so uncritical for so long a time that misconceptions about its nature and purposes grew, and unrealistic expectations about its intentions became embedded in institutional planning. If the relationship between the federal government and research universities has soured in recent years, at least part of the explanation can be found in those misconceptions and false expectations.

To put the matter bluntly, too many scientists and university officers came to believe that the government-university relationship was somehow exempt from ordinary rules of democratic politics. To say that is not to be especially critical. It is simply another way of observing that few of us are so ruthlessly analytical as to question the reasons for the good fortune that comes our way. It is much more common to conclude simply that it is ours because we deserve it.

That attitude was virtually universal among scientists and nearly so among university administrators. The record shows few warnings that doing business with government—especially a democratic government—is inevitably political; that the relationship between government and the interests that make up society is based, to a significant degree, on calculations of mutual advantage; and that government is an unstable ally precisely because those calculations are subject to rapid change as the public perception of the priority due to particular social problems shifts. A fair reading of the record will show that research and higher education had an unusually long run of governmental favor and that, in fact, they have not really fallen from favor so much as they have suffered from increased competition for it. To be precise, funding for academic research and development grew (in constant 1972 dollars) at an annual rate of 12 percent from 1953 to 1960, 14 percent from 1960 to 1968, zero percent from 1968 to 1974, and 4 percent from 1974 to 1978. Fifteen years of such high rates of growth is an extraordinary record of abundance, a record that made the drop to zero both shocking and unconscionable. The small real increases of recent years rank academic research and development as among the more favored of the discretionary objects of governmental patronage. Even the FY 1982 budget, the most stringent and controversial in memory, gave relatively favored treatment to most research programs.

The dominant view in university and scientific circles tends to be rather different. That view is best expressed in the image of partnership, perhaps the single metaphor most commonly used to describe the relationship of government to research and research training. A recent report from the University of California described the idea of partnership in this way:

> The partnership that evolved was a complex mix of many types of institutional and individual relationships. It was based on mutual interest and benefits and depended on agreement about the importance of research and the interrelationship between research and education. It depended too on a common perception of the responsibilities of each to sustain the relationship and preserve the special character of the universities. Ultimately it depended on a mutual recognition that scientific research and scholarship, because they enrich the lives of the American people in many ways, are of public interest and benefit.[2]

It is an attractive image, for genuine partners to an enterprise have common interests, work closely and cooperatively together, and are mutually supportive. But it is also a misleading image, for true partners—in the business sense, for example—have a shared commitment to a common goal, a shared responsibility based on mutual interest for the well-being of the enterprise, and each partner will suffer in precisely defined measure in the case of default

---

[2] *Partnership Between Universities and the Federal Government; Response to a Study of Federal Assistance Management Pursuant to the Federal Grant and Cooperative Agreement Act of 1977* (Berkeley: University of California Press, 1980), p. 7.

of obligation. None of those is true for the government-university relationship. In the nature of things, government cannot be a true partner. Its commitments are always contingent (frequently no more than annual) and are subject to short- or long-run changes depending on circumstances that have nothing to do with the terms or conditions of the "partnership." In the coldest and clearest view of the matter, research universities have no more claim to "partnership" with the government than do farmers, merchant shippers, highway builders, or any other group that has established a claim on government patronage. The government can be, and often is, at one and the same time a patron, adversary, buyer, and regulator. What it cannot be, in any sense that can be relied upon, is a partner.

Much of the bitterness over the deterioration of relations between government and research universities that marks the present climate can be traced to a conviction among the latter of betrayal, deriving from the belief that this relationship was somehow different from all others. In some of its details, that was undoubtedly true, but in its fundamentals it could not be. Sound future policies and the prospects for good relations in the future depend on a clear-eyed formulation of what agencies in the society are responsible, and in what measure, for insuring that these invaluable and irreplaceable institutions are able to perform at top effectiveness over a long period of time.

The main elements of such a formulation are clear enough. It must surely include frank recognition that the maintenance of a vital research enterprise in the country is unthinkable without the active involvement of the government. It must also include recognition of the inherent instability of that involvement, both as to its total at any moment and as to the components of the total, and therefore it must seek ways to limit institutional dependency on the stability of government funding. It must include a reaching out for new patrons and new alliances. The United States still retains a vital private sector which derives important benefits from the work of research universities.

New ways need to be devised to make business, in particular, a more active participant in the activities of research and training.

Finally, such a formulation must be explicit that the primary responsibility for maintaining the vitality of the research university rests with the faculties, administrators, and trustees who hold them in stewardship during their tenures in office. This is more than mere rhetoric. Dependency can sap responsibility, and in this case the ordinary dangers of excessive dependency on a major patron are exacerbated by the extent to which this patron—the public through its government—has come habitually to depend on the research university to solve its problems—defense, space exploration, disease, health care, and now industrial productivity and innovation. The urgency that such needs bespeak and the pressures they generate for fast results can be so overpowering as to distort institutional purposes, unbalance programs, and compromise high standards of quality. To avoid those results will require strong institutional agendas combined with strong instruments for defining collective institutional interests. Those responsibilities cannot be given to others except at great cost.

None of this necessarily foreshadows disaster. The American research university has become a remarkably productive institution, host to a large number of creative people whose work pushes back the boundaries of ignorance and helps distribute the benefits of knowledge. The task of policy today and tomorrow is to produce the conditions that will sustain them in their work. To be successful in that task will require movement in two directions. The first is toward finding ways of living with a powerful governmental patron by limiting the damage that the power of patronage can cause. The second direction leads toward the involvement of new nongovernmental patrons and the deeper and more profound involvement of old ones.

The chapters that follow may be seen as having in common a search for ways to move in those directions. Each chapter deals with a separate topic of importance to the re-

the policymaking arena in competition with a host of other claims. In an unstable world, the outcome of that kind of competition will, itself, be less than stable.

Clearly, the system that produces policy in the United States did not grow out of a passion for neatness or a strong attachment to orderly deliberative processes. The values it exalts are those of limited and dispersed power, and since in another arena those are the same values that support a strong and diverse set of educational institutions that remains relatively free of the most crippling forms of governmental control, there is little to be gained from lamenting the absence of more coordinated planning and policy. But neither is there anything to be gained by ignoring the dislocations that can be produced by policies which consist of ad hoc solutions to separate problems. There are costs attached to that way of doing business, and they bear heavily on institutions whose central activities are, by their very nature, continuous, long term, and not well adapted to sudden stops and starts.

Government policies with respect to advanced graduate training are a case in point. The driving force behind those policies in the whole of the postwar period—the perceived need that was most effectively translated into a political demand—has been the need for highly trained manpower in specifically identified fields of study.

That is, perhaps, not surprising. Nor, indeed, is it wholly inappropriate. The national government is not responsible, nor does anyone want it to be, for the fundamental sustenance of universities. Government policies from the time of the Morrill Act of 1862 have aimed at using universities for the achievement of other national purposes, while concern for their well-being as institutions has been sporadic and largely derivative of other goals.

To recognize that as the normal condition of public policy is not to applaud all of its consequences, nor should it lead to a lessening of efforts to ameliorate the worst of them. From the point of view of those responsible for the conduct of the major graduate schools, the worst of the consequences, by far, is the off-again/on-again quality of policies based on threatened shortages of manpower in one or another category. It is essential that those who make policy understand the effect of their actions on the institutions upon which the success of their policies depends. At the least, the injunction to do no harm may then be heeded, and the possibility of a more effective set of policies may be increased.

What is the harm, and what approaches might lead to better policies? The core of the matter lies in seeing fully the elements that make up the university. In its full range the modern research university is engaged in undergraduate and graduate teaching, research, and professional training. Furthermore, and distinctively, these are not isolated activities; at least the first three of them are conducted by the same faculty, and to a growing degree the fourth is becoming linked to the others.

By now, the intimate connection between graduate education and research is well understood. Most people who attend to such matters agree that the training for research is best done by those who are themselves actively engaged in the process of acquiring knowledge and, further, that that process is improved when it is aided and criticized by those who are preparing themselves to engage in it.

The connection between research and graduate training and undergraduate education is less well understood or appreciated. To a significant degree, universities and their faculties are responsible for obscuring the relationship. The enormous flowering of research and graduate education that accompanied the growth of government funding in the 1950s and 1960s undoubtedly produced imbalances in the quality of attention, thought, and effort that was devoted to undergraduate teaching. But the most important sign is not quantitative. It is based rather on the fact that research and scholarship are essentially isolating activities. At their most sophisticated, they involve a high degree of specialization, and they are accessible only to those who have the prerequisite knowledge. Graduate education moves students in that same direction and, hence, separates them from their fellows in other fields and even more from the less focused interests of undergraduates. Indeed, the very structure of the university rests on discipline-based departments, which in turn represent a convenient organization of knowledge for further detailed and specialized exploration.

The consequences are evident. Efforts to establish contact between professional schools and the rest of the university have, until quite recently, had only mixed success. Humanists and engineers too often huddle together in separate corners of the campus, each viewing the other with suspicion on the basis of knowledge that is modest at best.

Perhaps it is unfair to single out universities. As a people, Americans appear to have lost the image of the world as a potentially harmonious whole made up of many members, each with a contribution to make to the welfare of the whole. It is scarcely likely that universities, reflecting the habits of society as they must do, can be wholly different from it. But in the universities there is an instrument at hand for producing corrections. It is the program of undergraduate education.

Many of the best universities in the land have been engaged in the last few years in debates over the shape and content of the curriculum for freshmen and sophomores. Those debates and the movement toward greater curricular structure that have emerged from them must be seen as reactions against the atomization of the university that marked the preceding period. In that period the impulse toward specialization served to justify a more general disinclination to believe that there was any core of knowledge or values that was essential to an educated person. The result in many institutions was, literally, *dis*-integration; the recent and current focus on undergraduate education reflects an underlying need for *re*-integration.

The American research university depends for its intellectual character on the interdependence of graduate and undergraduate education. That relationship is not subject to cyclical change although it has surely been affected from time to time by the intellectual fashion of the day. When it is functioning at its best, the university is an integrated whole, a harmonious and mutually reinforcing blend of undergraduate, graduate, and professional teaching and of research. In the real world, of course, that describes a goal toward which policy should point and a standard from which departures should be measured. Sustained inattention or excessive attention to one part of the whole will produce harm to the total enterprise. In the end, each can be healthy only if all are healthy.

Against this backdrop, the inadequacies of public policies with respect to graduate education stand out in sharp relief. It can be argued with some justice that all of higher education expanded too rapidly in the two decades following World War II. But the large increases in enrollment, research volume, and facilities in so short a time were not the product of a conscious plan, and in any case, the real world is often different from the cooler calculations of planners. When they differ, reality is likely to prevail. And so it should. Only an unreasoning attachment to an abstract model of desirable rates of change could reject the social gains produced by the extension of higher education in the postwar decades. It should be noted, however, that as it has affected graduate education, the legacy of that period is not wholly a happy one.

It is fair to say that public policy dealt with graduate education not as part of a whole but rather in terms of its instrumental value for other parts of the system. Here lay the origin of the manpower fixation that has dominated policy ever since. The number and size of graduate programs was assessed wholly in terms of how many Ph.D.'s would be needed to teach the growing undergraduate bodies and to man the laboratories built and operated by government research funds. Those were in fact important considerations, and any acceptable set of policies had to account for them. By themselves, however, they were deficient, for when it became clear that undergraduate enrollments would enter a period of decline and that research dollars would no longer grow at the accustomed rate, the response with respect to graduate education was virtually automatic: cut back drastically. Since the growth of graduate programs was not grounded in any conception of an integrated university—not in Washington, in state capitals, or on many campuses—neither was their contraction. Furthermore, in the absence of fundamental change in the basis of public policy, the future is perfectly predictable: it will be marked by sudden spurts of forced growth in fields that come to be seen in short supply and equally sudden contraction when the supply is seen to equal or exceed the demand. That pattern has marked many fields of engineering in the past, and its almost perfect paradigm can be found in government policy toward medical education.

The trouble with that approach is that it takes more than entering students to create a high-quality graduate program. The accumulation of faculty, of library materials, of research facilities and equipment—those are all long-term developments. They do not disappear as the number of graduate students diminishes, and they cannot be called back into being should they be suddenly needed again. Adjustments are, of course, frequently possible; universities are not, after all, static and rigid systems, and so good people find other useful things to do. But to find virtue in adversity is not to advertise adversity as a virtue.

THE ELEMENTS OF POLICY

Instability in graduate education produces instability elsewhere in the university. Changes in enrollment at the graduate level affect both undergraduate teaching and research, and sudden changes are the most difficult to absorb. Sensible policy, that is, policy that pays heed to the health of institutions, would take care to make inevitable transitions as orderly as possible. How might that be achieved?

Enrollment: Quality of Students and Rates of Change

The key to returning stability to graduate education lies in avoiding sudden, sharp shifts in enrollment. Changes occur naturally enough over time as individual career choices respond to changing intellectual currents and economic realities. Educational programs can adapt to changes produced by those forces. Indeed, they constitute healthy signs of flexibility in the economic, social, and educational systems. But the dislocations produced by directed change, the ups and downs induced by the manipulation of external financial aid programs, are far more disruptive. Changes of that kind cannot be avoided altogether, but their effects can be mitigated. Since government actions have come to dominate the rate of change in graduate enrollments, it is appropriate first to attend to government policy.

The Support of Excellence

The most important long-term goal of government policy should be to assure that an adequate fraction of the most able college graduates is able to pursue graduate study. The number may vary somewhat over time as fiscal constraints change, as special purpose fellowship programs wax and wane, and as other conditions change. The programs to achieve this purpose are already in place. The competitive graduate fellowship awards by the National Science Foundation enable excellent science students to attend the university of their choice. The National Graduate Fellowship Program authorized by the Higher Education Act of 1980 would provide similar opportunities for students in other fields. That program authorizes 450 four-year awards annually. The NSF program, through 1981, was supporting 515 new students each year.

Those numbers are not adequate for the health of the system, but even so they are misleading. The National Graduate Fellows Program has not been funded, and the Reagan administration's proposed budget for FY 1982 would have closed out the NSF program by ending all new awards. That did not happen, but the very fact that so long-standing and fundamental a pillar of the nation's science education program was threatened underscores the need to remake the case for it and others like it.

That case does not rest on predictions of particular prospective shortages. It is based on a consideration that transcends estimates of specific needs. We have learned in the last quarter-century that the conditions of modern life require the availability of some adequate number of exceptionally able people who are trained as well as they can be. We need these people because we know that very able and well-trained people will find problems to solve. We know that the problems will be there—in universities, government service, business and industry, and in a host of other settings. What we cannot be certain of is that the problem solvers will be there. A strong Ph.D. program in a first-class university is the most rigorous intellectual training our educational system provides. Sound policy would assure that this training be used for first-class students.

In addition to the immediate budgetary pressures that stand in the way of such a proposal, programs of the sort just described have in the past proven vulnerable to the charge that they are "elitist," that their effect is to cluster the best students into a small number of institutions whose prestige and national visibility make them magnets for students whose fellowships enable them to choose the university they wish to attend. The arithmetic of the charge is accurate. The experience of competitive programs in which the winners may go where they wish shows quite clearly that a relatively few institutions end up with a relatively large share of the students. In political terms that has always been a liability since there are bound to be more institutions in more places that do not attract students than there are those that do. Since politics in a representative democracy is frequently best understood in terms of simple arithmetic, the problem is clear. Moreover, the problem is made worse by this country's long-standing love-hate relationship with the idea of quality. It is a genuinely difficult matter, and no other society of such size and complexity has ever tried over so long a period of time to grapple with it. No matter how much effort is devoted to assuring that all competitors—be they students, institutions of higher learning, business enterprises, baseball teams, or whatever—reach the starting line at the same time and that they play by the same rules, some will finish ahead of others.

It is widely believed that the approach urged here is unrealistic. So it is if the only measure of realism is the prospect for immediate fulfillment. It just may be, however, that an unabashed assertion of the value of high-quality education for the most able students can create a new set of prospects and thus a revised calculation of what is realistic. Much may be gained in the effort and little is to be lost.

There is no "solution" to the conflict, no easy way of splitting the difference and making everyone at least a little bit happy. The large graduate student support programs of the 1950s and 1960s in fact did just that through sheer numbers. But funding on such a scale is unlikely to recur, and so difficult decisions need to be made. Having passed through a long period of program building, it is now time to focus attention on the need to enable the best students to find the programs that are best for them. The sensible strategy, given scarce resources and the social return from high-quality education, is to subsidize students of quality.

Special Needs

Even if the foregoing proposal were to be adopted as policy, two immediately pressing problems would need to be addressed separately. The first is the need to attract more minority students to programs of graduate education, and the second is the need to assure an adequate supply of highly trained engineers. Despite extraordinary efforts in the last decade, the number of minority students entering graduate programs in many fields is still disappointingly low, as is their rate of entry into college and university faculties. It is a problem compounded both of social patterns in American society over many years and of current problems in graduate education. Whatever the causes, if the students who enter graduate school do not include increased numbers of high-quality minorities, the quality of future undergraduate teaching will have been compromised and we will have perpetuated the social patterns that we have been at such pains nationally to alter.

The point needs to be stressed. The basic principles that govern the career choices of minority college graduates are not fundamentally different from those that apply to other students. A decision to choose medical, law, or business training is neither irrational nor antisocial. What does seem clear, however, is that this nation has assumed the goal of universal access to higher education as one of its most important domestic responsibilities. The disenfranchised in the past have been disproportionately people of color. The national goal cannot be reached unless that pattern changes, and it is unlikely to change markedly unless college and university faculties change accordingly.

The fact that it will take years to make significant changes in faculties argues for a prompt beginning that includes at a minimum the removal of financial barriers for minorities so that at the very least the cost of lengthy graduate education is not added to the financial disadvantage of a teaching career compared with that of other professions.

The prevailing view of the law as expressed in the Bakke decision admits the use of racial and ethnic diversity as a legitimate educational criterion in making admissions to graduate and professional schools. Adequate financial assistance is needed to make real what is now both legitimate and necessary. One main federal program exists for that purpose, the Graduate and Professional Opportunities Program (GPOP). It has been in existence for three years. It is time to take account of that experience and to make changes in order to make it stronger.

The GPOP should be fully funded. For the academic year 1980–1981, new starts in that program were reduced from 550 to 213, a clearly inadequate number.

The administration of the program should accord better with the reality of recruitment. Specifically, allotments to institutions should not be limited to narrowly circumscribed fields but should be available for the support of the best minority students in the institution's applicant pool. That can be accomplished under a system of institutional allotments, but only if decisions about which institutions are to have fellowships are made with rigorous adherence to high standards of academic quality. The best assurance that good students will go to the institutions best suited to their talents lies in a system of nationally competitive awards, which the winners carry to the institutions of their choice. The National Science Foundation's Minority Graduate Fellowship Program is a small (forty-eight new awards for 1980–1981) but promising start in the right direction. The Department of Education should work toward a similar program in order to signal clearly its commitment to the best training for the best students, majority and minority.

The provision of engineering manpower is another special case. A high-technology modern society has a voracious appetite for engineers, but at least in the United States the appetite, like all appetites, diminishes when it is fed and increases when it is not.

Thus, it has long been the case that engineering is among the most market-sensitive of all academic areas. When the demand for engineers in industry is high, undergraduate enrollments increase rapidly, and the competition to hire graduates raises salaries and encourages some students who otherwise might have pursued advanced training to choose the more immediate economic rewards available to them.

We appear to be in such a period now.[1] Engineers are in short supply and computer specialists are the most sought after of all. In accordance with the usual pattern, undergraduate enrollments are rising rapidly, engineering and computer graduates are being attracted to industry by high salaries, and concern is being expressed about the ability of

---

[1] There is reason to be tentative about that as about all projections of manpower shortages. The anecdotal evidence strongly suggests shortages of engineers and computer specialists at all levels and especially for those with advanced training. On the other hand, the most comprehensive study to date is much more restrained. *Science and Engineering Education for the 1980s and Beyond*, published in October 1980 by the National Science Foundation and the Department of Education, concludes that

with a few exceptions, there should be adequate numbers of engineers and scientists at all degree levels to fill available positions in 1990—*provided* we assume that the nation does nothing different in the future in the ways it trains and makes use of engineers and scientists to address national problems. Since the technological complexity of our society is almost certain to increase, however, we believe that taking that assumption as a given would not be in the best interests of the nation. (pp. xxiii–xxiv)

One can only be tentative about policy judgments that rest on such a shifting foundation.

Ph.D. programs to meet the need for teachers. An added edge is lent to that concern by the fact that about half of the students now enrolled in engineering doctoral programs are foreign nationals, most of whom will not enter the academic job market.

Before embarking on a course of action that would repeat the boom-and-bust cycle of advanced training that is so damaging to institutions, it would be wise to consider other ways of providing an ample supply of Ph.D.'s in technological fields. One way is to recognize that this market swing, like others that have preceded it and still others that will follow, will be of limited duration. It is likely to produce at least part of the necessary adjustments by its own dynamics.

Second, to the extent that remediation of the particular problem may be needed, it may be partly achieved by intelligently conceived alliances between universities and industry. It is in the interest of industry to have an ample supply of first-rate people in the classrooms and laboratories of the engineering schools. Fellowship support for graduate students and subsidized programs of advanced training for engineers employed in industry are tested ways of helping able students get advanced training that equips them for careers in teaching and research. Once they are trained, the question of career choice is a much more complicated one, the answers to which depend finally on individual judgments that are a compound of financial, personal, and intellectual components. If there is a problem in assuring an adequate supply of teachers of engineering, its solution lies in making the academic career attractive in all of those dimensions.

Finally, it may truly be the case that careful monitoring will demonstrate that market processes together with imaginative alliances between industry and graduate training programs will leave an unacceptably large gap and that government programs in support of high technology Ph.D.'s are called for. In that event, by far the best way to achieve the purpose would be through the expansion of the NSF Graduate Fellowship Program through which the ablest students are matched automatically to programs that can accommodate them without expansion that will at a later date become unused capacity.

Research Assistantships

Government support for the education of graduate students has four main components: loans, for which graduate students are eligible along with all others; fellowships, awarded either in prize competition or on the basis of allotment to institutions; traineeships, allotted competitively to academic departments and awarded by them to individuals; and research assistantships, which are charged as a direct cost of research grants and contracts.

The last of those, the research assistantship, is critical to research and education in the sciences. It is, indeed, the embodiment of what has come to be the core of the American conception of the relationship between research and education for research, namely, that both are done better when they are done together. When research funds are in short supply, both sponsoring agencies and universities will look for ways to do the same work for less money. In the competition that ensues, the need for graduate student funding may not fare well when pitted against more immediately pressing needs, and that fact may come to be reflected in institutional practices and in government policies. Our recommendation here takes the form of a caution, that the pressures of the moment not be allowed to weaken the link between research and training that has made the American research university the enviably distinctive institution it has become.

The foregoing proposals are directed to the policies of government. Their overriding purpose is to assure a measure of continuity in the funding of graduate education in order to protect the entire university from the adverse consequences of instability in one of its component parts. It is important to note that to argue for continuity and stability is not to prejudge the necessity of expansion or contraction. Nor is it to wish for a world free of changing needs and pressures. It is, rather, to assert that frequent sudden changes of direction are harmful to the enterprise and that both growth and shrinkage should be managed with that truth in mind.

The Prospects for Young Scholars

The health and vitality of graduate education is inevitably associated with the prospects for constructive employment of new Ph.D.'s. A number of essentially separate developments have conspired to produce cause for concern. It is now clear that in the 1980s there will be fewer job openings on university faculties than at any time since the end of the war. The brew that has produced this result consists of the following:

1. The level of academic employment has always been strongly linked to the requirement for undergraduate teaching. Declining college enrollment in the next decade will limit employment opportunities.
2. In a parallel development, the low rates of growth in research funding, assuming that the recent trend continues, will yield few incremental opportunities.
3. Because of low rates of faculty growth in the 1940s and the very high rates in the 1950s and 1960s, college and university faculties now consist of unusually large proportions of faculty between the ages of forty and fifty. Thus, replacement opportunities through retirement will be fewer in the next decade than might ordinarily be expected.
4. Finally, law and policy governing the retirement of faculty are very much in flux. What seems likely is that changes in the law which raise the age of mandatory retirement will combine with the erosion by inflation of prospective pension benefits to produce a later average retirement age than in the past.

There have been several recent studies of this issue.[2] The most recent and most thorough was conducted by the

---

[2] An excellent summary of the main reports, as well as a review of the issue, is contained in "Smoothing Out the Flow of Young Scientists into Universities," by Margaret S. Gordon, Supplement J to the Final Report of the Carnegie Council on Policy Studies in Higher Education, *Three Thousand Futures: The Next*

Commission on Human Resources of the National Research Council (NRC). Taking into account the factors noted above, it concluded that in the fields of science and engineering, "there is a shortage in new openings of . . . about 600 positions per year at the Ph.D.-granting institutions." That condition is likely to persist until the late 1990s, by which time retirement rates should reach steady state and undergraduate enrollments are expected to rise.[3]

There is no serious dispute about the intrinsic undesirability of a condition in which faculties spend nearly two decades growing old together while talented young people are unable to bring their skills and fresh perspectives to the tasks of teaching and research. Moreover, the consequences of that condition will be especially unhappy for the effort to bring more women and minorities on to college and university faculties.

Nor is there dispute over the broad arithmetic of the issue or the projections that derive from it. In its fine detail, of course, the matter becomes a good deal more complex. Some fields will be more affected than others, some institutions more than others, some departments within institutions more than others. The refracted nature of the effects is a serious obstacle to framing sound and effective policies to meet the problem. So, too, is the fact that it is easier to prove that fewer young persons will be added, in the aggregate, to university faculties in the next two decades than in the last two than it is to prove that that fact is harmful to the condition of education and research. To its credit, the NRC study confronted that fact head on, and its candor lends weight to its conclusion:

While we have pointed to a number of factors relating the

Twenty Years for Higher Education (San Francisco: Jossey-Bass Inc., 1980), pp. 385–390.

[3]Commission on Human Resources, *Research Excellence Through the Year 2000: The Importance of Maintaining a Flow of New Faculty into Academic Research* (Washington, D.C.: National Academy of Sciences, National Research Council, 1979), p. ii. "Steady state" is defined as "a situation of balance between numbers recruited into and numbers leaving academic positions, with a stable total faculty size and unchanging age distribution" (p. 16).

flow of young researchers to research vitality, we have put little emphasis in our analysis on the premise that young researchers are, as a class, uniquely creative or productive. In our view, a steady flow of "new blood" and in part "young blood" into academic departments is important in large part because of its impact on the overall research environment of the department and on the maintenance of a generational mix conducive to good communication and the most effective motivation of successive cohorts of independent investigators. Some of the effects we have pointed to are subtle and indirect. They have not for the most part been quantified in the existing literature on the sociology of science—and perhaps some of them cannot be in the present state of the art. We believe further research on these questions to be highly desirable. But in the absence of definitive research, we have based our analysis on our experience and understanding of the functioning of the academic research system and on the testimony of other experienced observers. That experience leads us to believe that the vitality of academic science would be seriously impaired by sharp restrictions on the hiring of new faculty.[4]

RECOMMENDED POLICIES

To ignore such a warning would be imprudent in the extreme. But to know how intelligently and effectively to heed it is equally difficult. Indeed, the most recent careful look at this topic, that of the National Commission on Research, concludes that "even the most careful manpower projections are too narrow and unconfident to be a sound basis for planning."[5] The commission therefore decided to make no recommendations on this topic.

Perhaps it is best to start by being clear about the goal of policy. Here as elsewhere, the most important goal should be to help institutions protect themselves against the consequences of instability. It is important to be clear about this. Any set of policies whose aim is to insulate individu-

---

[4] Ibid., pp. 65–66.
[5] National Commission on Research, *Research Personnel: An Essay on Policy* (Washington, D.C., 1980).

als or institutions from the effects of real, long-term social change is bound to fail. Furthermore, policies of that kind are self-defeating because they inhibit the working of the adaptive mechanisms that are built into strong social systems. However, it is an important and legitimate goal of policy to mitigate the damaging disruption that can be produced by too rapid rates of change.

If the goal of policy is to smooth the transition from one set of conditions to a radically different set, then the substance of policy must account for the fact that the new conditions have been produced by several independent, though converging, causes. Thus, efforts at mitigation need to be tailored to the circumstances that have produced the need for them. Viewed in that way, proposals for mitigation group themselves naturally into several categories.

☐ *Retirement Policies.* There should be no further increase in the minimum age for mandatory retirement. In 1982, college and university faculty are subject to the federally set floor of age seventy for mandatory retirement. In enacting that floor, the Congress wisely allowed a three-year grace period before applying it to tenured faculty. It is important that the effects of the change be absorbed and evaluated before further changes are made.

As economic conditions permit, institutional programs of voluntary early retirement for faculty should be extended. In an inflationary period, the economic incentives for retirement diminish and the cost of providing realistically for early retirement increases. Early retirement programs also risk encouraging retirement by the most active and productive senior faculty rather than the least. Notwithstanding those two serious obstacles, institutions should assess their ability to renew their faculties with younger persons; and where that ability appears too low, they should give high priority to generous early retirement programs.

☐ *The Enhancement of Existing Faculty.* The primary resource for teaching and research under any conceivable set of circumstances for the next twenty years will be those between the ages of about thirty and fifty who now hold faculty positions. The success of that group in maintaining its vitality and productivity will be the single most important determinant of the quality of teaching and research for the remainder of this century. The universities themselves must take the responsibility for developing programs and attitudes that encourage intellectual growth and change by faculty. No single model exists, and each institution will need to search for the ways that best fit its circumstances and traditions. Refreshment can come from activities that range from released time for the development of new courses to a change of intellectual focus, faculty seminars on topics that bridge specialist lines, and others that thought and imagination will produce.

Private foundations and industry should attend to the financing of thoughtful and imaginative institutional programs of faculty refreshment. Some already have made grants for that purpose. Others will find it an especially rewarding object of philanthropy.

☐ *Academic and Nonacademic Careers.* A great deal more systematic attention should be given to the generation of career patterns in which scholars and scientists will move among universities, industry, government, and other nonprofit institutions. In fact, a great deal of this kind of movement takes place in the natural course of events but almost always as unique events in the life of separate individuals; rarely is it seen as a phenomenon whose benefits might be increased by better planning.

The opportunities are especially rich in the fields of science and engineering that are likely to see greater collaboration between universities and business. In another context we have noted that the fear among academics that good scientists may be attracted to industry is misplaced, that movement of that kind is evidence that the social system called science is healthy, not that the university part of it is ailing. If those movements can be seen, and even planned, as parts of careers that will move in and out of the academy over time, then additional career opportunities will become available because the range of what is considered appropriate academic employment will be enlarged.

We see no easy solution to the problems that will be caused by a diminishing university market for young faculty. The conditions that are creating the problems are known and fixed. It is conceivable, of course, that the future may bring another major expansion of government research funding, but there are no signs of that in sight, and it would hardly be prudent to plan in the hope that it will happen. What is required is the necessary but unglamourous task of spotting approaching trouble, by field and by institution, and then with imagination taking such steps as may be possible to smooth the period of transition.

This is an especially appropriate area for foundation giving. Several foundations have already made grants which will enable universities to anticipate forthcoming retirements by bringing in young faculty before a retirement occurs, and others which will provide research opportunities for young faculty. Three notable examples are the Sloan Foundation, which has long been active in the support of young scientists, and, more recently, the Andrew W. Mellon Foundation and the Northwest Area Foundation, which have made significant grants to help institutions bring young people on to their faculties earlier than would otherwise be possible.

Stimulating foundations, including, of course, industry foundations, to become active in this area is preferable to seeking new government appropriations for that purpose. Foundations are better able to target programs to specific points of urgent need than is the government; they are less likely to be intrusive into academic processes—an especially important consideration when money is used to pay faculty salaries—and foundations are better able to look at total institutional needs, including those in the social sciences and the humanities, than is the government.

It is appropriate to close with an emphasis on careers, for it is only by holding out the prospect of intellectually rewarding careers that the research universities can compete successfully for what they will need most: a fair share of the best and most creative people available. Achieving that goal will require strategies that may include, but will surely be larger than, specific programs of pre- or postdoctoral fellowships and similar efforts. It will require the availability of facilities, equipment, and library resources that make possible the doing of research at the most advanced levels; it will require the presence of stimulating colleagues and good students; and it will demand creative work, not the demands of a spurious accountability.

The movement of very good people into industry need not be viewed as a loss to the universities but as a long-term gain for society. But what should be a social gain can quickly become a loss if the best people flee from the academic world because that environment is no longer hospitable to the kind of creative work which has always been its main attraction to people of quality.

CHAPTER THREE

INDUSTRY-UNIVERSITY COLLABORATION:
The New Partnership

The 1970s produced many shocks to U.S. self-esteem. Not the least of them came from the growing awareness that American industry and the technology on which it is based were losing ground in the competition with Western Europe and Japan. By 1980, both in absolute and relative terms, the U.S. economy needed help. Indicators of the decline are not hard to find. A recent study listed the following:

1. Between 1966 and 1976, the U.S. patent balance decreased with respect to the United Kingdom, Canada, West Germany, Japan, and the USSR. By 1975 it was negative for the last three.
2. The proportion of the world's major technological innovations produced by the United States decreased from 80 percent in 1956–1958 to 59 percent in 1971–1973.
3. The real Gross Domestic Product per employed civilian decreased in the United States relative to France, West Germany, Japan, the United Kingdom, and Canada between 1960 and 1977.
4. The United States moved to last place in terms of gains in relative productivity (output/manpower) in the manufacturing industries in comparison with France, West Ger-

many, Japan, the United Kingdom, and Canada between 1960 and 1977.[1]

It is clear that many thoughtful people are beginning to place their hopes for improvements in the competitive position of American business and in the health of university-based science in the growing collaboration between business and universities. The best time to be thoughtful about those links is at the start when they are still malleable so that what is learned from early experience can be used to improve later practice and so that unreasonable expectations do not lead to disappointment and disenchantment.

Few subjects have received as much attention recently in university circles as the prospect of closer relations with American business. Announcements of bilateral arrangements, as for example between Harvard and Monsanto and between MIT and Exxon, have been scrutinized with great interest and examined for what they may augur. Much is written,[2] meetings are held, and a general air of optimism and hope prevails.

Interest in business is high as well. Declining productivity, an apparent lag in industrial innovation, and increasingly disadvantaged comparisons with the vibrant economies of Western Europe and Japan have combined to focus attention on research as an important source of innovation and consequently on research universities as the main suppliers of high-quality research and of those who are trained to do it.

Nor has government been inactive. Moved by a sluggish economy and by the growing comparative disadvantage of

---

[1] Arthur Levine and Rachel Volberg, "A Comparative Review of Scholarly, Scientific, and Technological Progress in the United States," Supplement J to the Carnegie Council on Policy Studies in Higher Education, *Three Thousand Futures: The Next Twenty Years for Higher Education* (San Francisco: Jossey-Bass Inc., 1980), p. 347. The data are from U.S. National Science Board, *Science Indicators,* 1976 and 1978.

[2] The recent report of the National Commission on Research, *Industry and the Universities: Developing Cooperative Research Relationships in the National Interest* (Washington, D.C., August 1980), is especially useful both for its discussion of issues and for its recommendations.

American business in relation to foreign competitors, a variety of government units, including the Department of Commerce, the National Science Foundation, the Office of Science and Technology Policy, and several committees of Congress have been studying policies, programs, and organizational arrangements that might improve the means of moving research into practice.

Fortunately, history provides grounds for optimism. One of the qualities that distinguishes the history of American higher education from that of other nations is the strong orientation of the American academy toward the world of affairs. That statement may have an odd ring to contemporary ears because in recent years more public attention has been devoted to reports of antagonism or estrangement between the two. As summarized in a recent, thoughtful study of the conditions of academic science:

> Although hard evidence is lacking, there are reasons to believe that the links between universities and industry weakened in the two decades following World War II and approached their nadir in the early 1970s. The principal factors behind the decline appear to have been: (1) the separation of academic research from perceived industrial needs; (2) the decreased interest among Ph.D.'s and other graduates in industrial research, and (3) the relative decline of basic research in industry.[3]

Even during this period, however, universities and industry were by no means strangers to one another. Corporate philanthropy grew, consulting by university faculty was widespread, and some institutions had extensive and productive associations with industry. The Research Triangle Park in North Carolina and the Stanford Industrial Park are notable examples of such interaction.

These connections derive from an older and more enduring tradition. For example, not only did the Land Grant Act establish a remarkably fruitful relationship

---

[3]Bruce L. Smith and Joseph J. Karlesky, *The State of Academic Science: The Universities in the Nation's Research Effort* (New York: Change Magazine Press, 1977), p. 62.

between an important university sector and American agriculture, but its twin purpose, namely, to improve instruction and training in the "mechanic arts," was equally successful, both in its own right and by example to other institutions. Much of the technical talent that developed and operated the technological infrastructure of American industry has been university-trained, and in recent years the same can be said for much of the managerial talent as well.

Furthermore, it is useful to remember that the widespread acceptance of basic research, as measured by the number of people engaged in it and the resources devoted to it, is of quite recent origin. It is based on an act of faith that inquiry that is undertaken with no practical end in mind will in fact turn out to have practical value. That faith has been rewarded often enough in recent years to justify continued belief. But in the history of science, even quite recent history, it has been more the norm that fundamental discoveries have been by-products of research undertaken in order to solve a particular problem. The achievements of modern basic science are impressive enough to stand as their own justification. If, however, new alliances with industry should lend a more applied cast to some areas of university research, the record suggests that it will not be necessary to despair for the future of fundamental discovery.

Thus, although the foundation for new relationships exists, it is by no means clear yet what kind of structure can be erected on it. The answer to that question will be determined mainly by the actions of the university, business and industry, and the federal government. Each has much to gain from the growth of a successful collaboration and much to lose from the failure of one to develop. If the policies that each adopts mesh, then success is likely. Therefore, it is important to be thoughtful, while the relationship is still in its formative stages, about the policies that are most likely to be successful and the conditions that are most likely to produce those policies. Let us look at each of the main actors, at what each wants, and at the policies that seem most likely to achieve their purposes.

THE RESEARCH UNIVERSITY OUTLOOK

The federal government has come to occupy such a pivotal position in the financing of basic research that the kindling of university interest in support from business and industry can be understood only in the context of the problems that have arisen in the primary government-university relationship. Those problems have to do with money and with more than money. Understanding this is essential to a full appreciation of the new collaboration.

There is no single authoritative statement of policy to which one can point, but the effect, de facto, of thirty years of government support of basic research in science and technology is to make the continuation of that support an accepted principle of public policy. While the principle has been established, so too has a refinement of it: the base will be protected, but there can be no reliable expectation about the rate of growth. That critical element will vary with the condition of the economy, the demands of competing social needs, and the winds of political fortune.

Basic research is primarily a public good. Its rewards are diffuse and unpredictable, and therefore there is a limit to which it is appropriate for profitmaking organizations to invest in it. Thus, no reasonable person expects that the support of university-based research by business will substitute for any significant part of the publicly provided base. But it is reasonable to work toward a level of business support that might buffer research programs from sudden, short-term losses and that in the longer term would provide resources for growth and improvement.

There is another important motivation of academic interest in business that derives from the experience with government. While it has to do with money, it is not primarily financial in character. Until World War II the financing of research in universities was almost wholly the responsibility of the private sector, agriculture excepted. The federal government now accounts for two-thirds of the funds spent for research and development in universities. The next largest contributors are the institutions themselves, followed by state governments. Industry and private foundations combined account for well under 10 percent of the total. Circumstances vary somewhat from field to field, but university-based scientific research now depends on annual appropriations from the federal government for its sustenance.

It certainly is not unusual for the government to have come to occupy a dominant position in an area that hitherto had been primarily a private responsibility. That, in fact, has been the trend in Western Europe for a century and in the United States for nearly half a century. In health care, old age security, and other social welfare fields, the government has also come to play a large and perhaps still growing role, but there remain in those fields significant private alternatives or complements to government programs. In the support of basic research the government blankets the field to an uncommon degree.

This condition has not come about by accident. Government support of research in universities grew out of World War II. It was the experience of the war that demonstrated the value of the university-based scientist and that provided the habit and the bureaucratic infrastructure to continue in a postwar period that was dominated by East-West confrontation and the cold war. Furthermore, science was increasingly expensive. Research in high-energy physics, for example, was clearly beyond the capacity of universities to support out of their own resources and clearly outside the reasonable sphere of interest of the private sector. But the same came to be true for biomedical research and many, if not most, aspects of technology.

Academic science could not have grown without large-scale support from the government. Furthermore, the continuation of high levels of government support is essential if science and technology in the universities, and hence in the nation, are to remain strong in the future. But there is ample evidence from history and contemporary experience to warn that excessive dependence on a single patron produces an unhealthy degree of vulnerability. This is true even when the patron is as internally diverse as is the federal bureaucracy. That diversity is an important safeguard of institutional freedom, but it can no longer be seen as wholly adequate. If the future is marked by increasing attempts within government to rationalize and make uniform the conditions of support—as in the current struggle over the meaning of "accountability" in the context of the cost reimbursement regulations—then the existence of a live private alternative and model can be critically important. Just as the existence of strong private colleges and universities has helped to establish norms of institutional autonomy that are of great value to public institutions, so can the existence of a large and enlightened private sector establish norms in research support.

The record of the private foundations suggests yet another important university interest in stimulating corporate research support. The foundations, in the fields of their interests, have long stood as a counterweight to the tendency of public programs to move toward broad and thin distribution of resources. In fact, the U.S. government's programs of research support have been as faithful to the principle of quality, as predicted by peer review, as it is possible for a representative government of continental scope to be. It is a proud record. However, it is important to recognize that the pressures to add distributional criteria to decisions are powerful, persistent, and, in the long run, to some degree effective. Individual corporations are subject to a variety of local pressures, but in the support of research and of the institutions capable of doing research, the collective example set by industry can serve as a reminder of the crucial importance of nurturing intellectual work of the highest quality.

The lessons learned about government in recent years have provided a powerful stimulus to campus interest in industry. By themselves, however, they do not constitute a wholly adequate explanation. A more complete picture must consider some other factors. For one, as the dominance of U.S. industry in world markets has been challenged, more sectors of industry have been forced to focus on product change and innovation, as opposed to finding ways of doing less expensively what one already does well. The chemical industry provides an instructive example of a general tendency among mature industries. At a recent meeting of leaders of the chemical industry and heads of university departments of chemistry and chemical engineering, M. E. Pruitt of Dow Chemical told the group that

> as the chemical industry has matured it has developed products and processes to defend. It has become more short term in its objectives. Management has become less firmly founded in technology, more business oriented. As a result, interest and funds for basic chemical research have dried up.[4]

Similar observations might equally well be made of the automobile and steel industries, among others.

Second, there is good evidence to support the conclusion that the quality of scientific instrumentation in university laboratories has fallen behind that found in the best industrial labs. Thus, university faculty stand to profit from the access to more modern equipment that collaboration with industry will bring. Finally, working more closely with industry can bring important advantages to graduate students and young scientists, both in terms of support for graduate study and in postdegree employment.

The most important requirement for successful collaboration between any business firm and any university is the existence of mutual respect among the scientists and engineers involved. There is a growing body of anecdotal evidence that suggests that major collaborative efforts are most likely to emerge from individual relationships between scientists, from which come the confidence that worthwhile work is possible on a larger scale.

For a very long time many university faculty have been either disdainful of or oblivious to much of the work of

---

[4] Cited in Michael Heylin, "Industry/Academic Cooperation: A Step Forward," *Chemical and Engineering News* 58 (September 29, 1980): 33.

industrial scientists. This is a widely known but little publicized condition. It is reflected in the concern current in some quarters that first-class scientists and engineers are being lured from university positions to industrial laboratories. In fact, such encouraging evidence of a genuinely flexible market for high quality intellectual talents should be applauded. Not the least of the reasons for that applause is the likelihood that having good people on both sides of the relationship will make it easier and more fruitful.

☐ Institutional policies with respect to such matters as patents and licenses and the handling of proprietary information and its implications for freedom of publication will need careful thought. At present, such policies vary widely among institutions, and perhaps that is as it should be. But an effort among institutions to consider issues of common interest—for example, freedom of publication—and to articulate broadly applicable standards about them would seem to be an early order of business. The Association of American Universities (AAU) should take the lead in defining the issues and bringing together the appropriate people.

☐ There is an immediate and pressing area of concern that can provide the first subject for such a gathering. That is the rapid proliferation of arrangements by individual scientists and by institutions to exploit the commercial applications of recombinant DNA and related technology. There are issues of urgent concern to universities as a group that are not necessarily accounted for by any individual arrangement or by the aggregate of all of them. To mention but one, though perhaps the most important, universities have a primary interest in keeping lines of scientific communication and collaboration as open and as free as possible. The expeditious advance of science depends on that openness. If the concern for commercial advantage were to discourage the prompt sharing of the results and products of basic research, then both science and its applications would suffer. Since it is the conduct of scientists that is primarily the issue here, the standards that govern conduct must, in the end, be defined by the scientists themselves. However, science takes place in institutions, and therefore institutional values are at stake too. The causes of both science and commerce will be better served if issues like this are discussed thoughtfully and openly in a setting that encourages the identification of shared interests. The AAU, representing the leading research universities of the nation, is strategically placed to provide that setting.

☐ Universities need to become more sophisticated in stimulating opportunities and shaping them appropriately. Scientists and administrators can bring to the connections with industry the same energy and imagination that have long characterized programmatic relations with government. It has never been the case that university science was simply the passive recipient of federal research dollars whose purposes were defined by the Washington bureaucracy. Rather, the process has properly been an interactive one in which scientists have played an active and frequently dominant part in establishing program directions. Even in programs sponsored by agencies with clearly defined missions, such as the Department of Defense and the National Aeronautics and Space Administration (NASA), the initiative in defining relevant scientific problems comes largely from the university scientists and engineers. Keeping the initiative there is perhaps the best guarantee of scientific vitality.

THE BUSINESS OUTLOOK

For nearly thirty years it has seemed safe to leave the nurturing of basic science to the processes that produce federal appropriations. Those processes no longer seem so reliable. It will take heightened sophistication on the part of business leadership to act on that recent understanding.

It is almost certainly the case, human nature being what it is, that more is expected from the interaction of business and the university than is likely to be delivered by either side. Certainly it is the case that university-based research

RICHARD G. COX LIBRARY
UN. OF SOUTHERN MISS. - GULF PARK

contains no major prescriptions for curing an ailing economy or for assuring profitability for any given business enterprise. It is, therefore, especially important that careful thought be given to defining reasonable expectations, a task that will require a mature understanding of what universities do well and what lies behind their capacity to do those things.

For most American businesses, indeed perhaps all, the single most important activity of colleges and universities, collectively, is the education and training of men and women to assume technical and managerial positions. Recognition of the importance of that function motivates much of the extraordinary amount of corporate philanthropy directed to institutions of higher education.

That fundamental interest, a concern for the continued supply of the best educated and most highly trained persons, can equally well justify business support of university-based research. The value to a firm of a relationship with a particular university laboratory may be high or low as measured by the amount of commercially applicable research it receives, but if properly managed, it is sure to be high if measured by access to able students. The premise on which the American research university rests is that research is better when it encompasses the education and training of students, and education and training are more rigorous and creative when they are done in the context of an active research program. It is the totality that provides the full measure of benefit; a more narrow calculus courts disappointment by adopting too narrow a definition of return on investment.

To risk a tautology, then, what research universities do best—and are almost alone in doing—is fundamental research and the training for research. Their ability to continue to perform these tasks is of crucial importance to the future well-being of industry as a whole although its relevance to the fortunes of any single firm may be difficult to discern at a particular moment. Lewis Thomas has written eloquently of the most recent example of the force of the truism. He reminds us:

Recombinant-DNA techniques could not have evolved without the thirty-year background of research in virology and molecular genetics, almost all of it done without the faintest inkling that anything like recombinant-DNA lay ahead.

Thomas goes on to argue:

We are beginning to draw from a bank of stored information in biomedical science, and I suspect that we are doing something like this in the physical sciences as well. There is some danger that the need to continue depositing new information in that bank will be overlooked in the pressure for quick applications. . . . The recent examples of marketable products from hybridoma antibodies and recombinant-DNA genomes ought to be raising new anxieties about this problem in the one segment of our society that has the greatest economic stake in basic science over the very long haul, that vast collection of industries known as Corporate America. They are or should be uniquely concerned, out of pure self-interest, for what will be available in the way of pure information in, say, the year 1995 or 2000, waiting then for application to new products. If long-term investments in basic science are not continued, they will find themselves out of business or, anyway, out of competition with their counterparts in other nations.[5]

It is perhaps oversimplified, but only slightly so, to observe that business has tended to concentrate on two kinds of interactions with the academic world. The first is broadly philanthropic. Its extent has grown substantially in recent decades, and it expresses the broadest interest of the business community in the health of colleges and universities. The second is more focused in that it rests on a view of institutions of higher learning as the producers of products of value. The most important of these are educated persons and research of more or less current utility.

These are two essential levels of interaction, and nothing should inhibit their further growth. But if "the bank of

---

[5]Lewis Thomas, "Science on Wall St.," *Science 80* (March–April 1980), pp. 22–24.

stored information" is not to be emptied, a third level needs to be added. At this new level the focus must be on maintaining and enhancing the capacity of universities to engage in fundamental research and scholarship.

The most productive research is likely to arise from relationships forged among scientists in one company and in one university. Those relations, multiplied many times, can form a strong collaborative network. But single-company-to-single-university connections are not sufficient by themselves. A productive research environment requires more than support for particular scientists who are doing work of interest to a sponsor. It requires support for young investigators beginning to develop their own lines of research; it requires start-up costs for lines of research not well enough proven to attract full support; it requires funds for keeping laboratory instrumentation up to date. In short, the work of the individual scientist or laboratory rests on a broad institutional capacity to support high-quality work. If that capacity is not to atrophy, the user of the final product must assume a share of the responsibility for maintaining it. There is a collective responsibility among users and beneficiaries to ensure the continuation of the enterprise on which they draw.

☐ Individual firms exercising enlightened funding policies can make important contributions to institutional flexibility. However, what is needed is systematic attention to that task, and that can be achieved only by rising above decisions of individual firms to industrywide decisions. Every industry whose member firms are active collaborators with universities should recognize and give effect to a shared responsibility to maintain the invisible institutional underpinnings of the universities on which they depend. It is not necessary nor is it especially desirable to specify the format that the assumption of this responsibility might take. If universities are varied and prize their differences, so too are the many elements of business and industry with which they interact. What is important is the recognition of the obligation.

During the most generous and most enlightened period

of government support for research, the government's responsibility for maintaining institutional capacity was embodied in such programs as the National Science Foundation's Institutional Improvement for Science Program and the Biomedical Research Support Grant of the National Institutes of Health. The former no longer exists, and the latter has shrunk under budgetary and other pressures. The flexibility that these programs provided enabled local decisions to be made about local needs. They provided valuable mitigation of the fragmentation that often accompanies project-by-project funding of research.

Corporate funds committed to this common effort should not be competitive with or subtracted from philanthropy. What is proposed here is philanthropic only as a metaphor—in the sense that any act of generosity that does not have an identifiable return associated with it may be called philanthropy. Rather, what is proposed is organization in pursuit of corporate interests that can only be achieved collectively.

It is especially encouraging to note the movement of the chemical industry toward an industrywide association in support of university programs of chemistry and chemical engineering.[6] The industry has established a Council for Chemical Research whose board of directors includes corporate and university representatives. The council, in turn, has set up a Chemical Sciences and Engineering Fund to which chemical firms will contribute money and from which grants will be made. Much will be learned from that experience about both the opportunities and the problems of collective action, and what turns out to be of generalizable value should be adapted to the particular circumstances of other industries. In other sectors, other forms will be more appropriate.

In a similar vein, it is important to recognize that the relationships that grow between individual firms and aca-

---

[6] See M. E. Pruitt, ed., *First Midland Conference on Advances in Chemical Science and Technology, October 15–17, 1979* (Midland, Mich.: Dow Chemical Co., 1980).

demic scientists and engineers are possible only because the university exists and makes possible scholarly work. The principle of full reimbursement of the indirect costs of research for which universities have for so long argued in the context of government funding rests at bottom on that fact. Too often, the dispute has taken the form of spats between rival accountants, but the core of the dispute is the insistence that the sponsor of research assume a responsibility for the less visible costs of maintaining the institution which makes the research possible. That principle of full recognition of indirect costs should be embedded in all industry-university research agreements.

THE GOVERNMENT OUTLOOK

The interest of government in enhancing productivity is understandable and appropriate. The involvement of government in the development of more extensive connections between research universities and industry is essential and inevitable. What is wholly problematic, however, is how best for the government to express its interest and what forms its involvement should take. The plain fact is that no one knows how to stimulate innovation or whether, indeed, it is any more likely to be legislated into being than is any other creative act. Nor is it clear what interventions, if any, will enhance the growth of productive relations between parties still searching for specific expressions of interests that they hold generally in common.

It is too soon, and experience is too limited, to know what will work and what will not. Therefore, the most useful contribution the government can make is to remove barriers to the new relationship and to add incentives thoughtfully and judiciously. It would seem to be premature to start large new programs to call innovation into being, and it is likely that the structures required to run such programs would, themselves, turn into obstacles to change. There is an appropriate role for government. The first steps in defining that role are encompassed in the following recommendations.

☐ Business should be provided with tax incentives for the support of research in universities. The internal revenue system, virtually from its birth, has made provision for incentives to encourage private spending for public purposes. The Tax Reduction Act of 1980 does provide favorable treatment to industry for incremental expenditures on research, but with no particular incentive to invest in university-based research. That incentive should be provided in the next tax bill. The enactment of such legislation would provide a valuable impetus to the growth of the desired relationships, and it would do so in a nondirective way, thereby assuring the maximum flexibility in finding the arrangements that are most suitable to the circumstances of the parties.

☐ The rules governing the assignment of patent rights for inventions made with the aid of government funding need to be made supportive of the aim of encouraging innovation as a major source of economic growth. It is generally recognized that the initial research is usually the least costly part of the process of translating ideas into marketable products or processes. The costs and the attendant risks accumulate as an idea moves from the germinal steps to development to more refined applications and finally into the marketplace. For that reason, the ability to hold a license for exclusive use of an invention is frequently crucial to the corporate decision to invest in the next stages.

Government policy with respect to who holds title to patents derived from government-sponsored research in university laboratories is currently in a state of confusion. Some agencies have allowed universities to patent and license such inventions; others have not. The growth of collaboration between industry and academic science would inevitably increase the mixing of public and private funds and of the ideas produced with their use. Thus, overly restrictive patent policies are likely to inhibit that growth.

The problem was addressed by the enactment of the University and Small Business Patent Act in the Ninety-sixth Congress. This legislation extends the principles of the Institutional Patent Agreements used by the Department of Health and Human Services to all government-sponsored research. Universities will thus be able to prosecute patents on inventions made in their laboratories with the use of public funds, subject to appropriate protection of the public's interest. The ability of universities to patent and license such inventions is an important step toward solving the problems produced by the use of public and private resources from the same laboratory. Regulations that will translate the new law into governmentwide practice have not yet been issued. It is essential that when they are, they further the law's purpose and not thwart it.

Very little is known about the kinds of arrangements most likely to produce fruitful associations between universities and industries. In some circumstances bilateral agreements may be sensible; in others, relations between a single university and several corporations may be productive; still others may be more suitable to industrywide support of a number of institutions. The government can play a useful role in helping to stimulate study of these various arrangements so that each may be used in its most appropriate setting.

In that context, the 1979 study undertaken by the Office of Science and Technology Policy[7] made a useful beginning. Welcome, too, was the decision of the National Science Board to make the topic of university–industry research relationships the subject of its 1981 annual report and of a similar study being conducted by the General Accounting Office.

If the first priority of government policy is to remove the obstacles to industry–university cooperation and the second to seek deeper understanding of the conditions under which such cooperation is likely to prosper, then the third priority must be self-restraint in the initiation of new programs that are intended to produce the cooperation under forced draft.

---

[7] See Denis J. Praeger and Gilbert S. Omenn, "Research, Innovation, and University-Industry Linkages," *Science* 207 (January 25, 1980): 379–384.

To be sure, there is good reason to believe that productivity is linked to scientific and technological innovation, that universities are a leading source of those valuable products, and that closer connections between universities and industry may help to move science research into practice. These are modest though very important premises for policy. But premature closure on the ways to bring their promise to fulfillment may succeed only in dampening the spirit of experimentation and the willingness to correct mistakes that so delicate a mission requires. A government program, once begun, is hard to stop or even to change. If the program involves the creation of a new organization, then the rigidity is compounded by the dynamics of organizational survival. Already, programs aimed at stimulating industry-university cooperation have been started by NASA, the Department of Defense, the Department of Energy, the Department of Commerce, and the National Science Foundation.

A particularly vivid example of the dangers of premature enthusiasm was seen in the introduction of the Small Business Innovations Research Act of 1979 in the Ninety-sixth Congress. Starting from the evidence that recent increases in innovation and productivity can be traced to relatively small firms in industries like electronics, this legislation would have required that every federal R&D agency increase its awards to small business by 1 percent per year either until the total reaches 10 percent of the agency R&D budget or until it has increased its R&D awards to small business by 5 percent, whichever is larger. Fortunately, testimony at congressional hearings pointed out the problems with the proposed legislation and helped to defeat it in committee. Unfortunately, a similar proposal was revived in the Ninety-seventh Congress with formidable support.

Since there is no reason to believe that such a drastic shift away from principles of scientific and technological merit in the award of research and development funds would produce better research or more innovation, the popularity of this legislation among congressmen can only be understood as the wish to do *something* in the hope that some benefit may be produced. The hope is misplaced and the legislation it spawned is misguided. It is important, though, as further testimony to the urgency of the nation's economic problems. At this stage, however, the soundest policy can be summed up in the Hippocratic injunction to physicians: do no harm. It may be that very little is required of government beyond removing existing obstacles and providing modest incentives. It may be that more direct approaches will be useful in some circumstances. Above all, however, it is essential to avoid impatience. The insistence on quick solutions and early results is likely to be destructive of the end to which it is directed. Some relationships cannot be willed into being, or purchased, or mandated. This is one such. If it is allowed to grow and be nurtured in appropriate ways, it is likely to last for a very long time, to the benefit of all.

CHAPTER FOUR

RESEARCH LIBRARIES:
Cooperation for Survival

Research university libraries and several notable nonuniversity private and public research libraries provide access to the materials on which scholarly research in all fields depends. They provide support for both undergraduate and graduate teaching, access and services to other libraries in their regions and nationally, and services to government, industry, and business. In their breadth and depth, they are unique repositories of the records of the intellectual and cultural history of civilization.

A revolution is now in process in the way these libraries provide service to their users. Although the great libraries were probably never as comprehensive and "universal" as faculty members and librarians wished them to be, the ideal of the research library until about the middle of this century was to develop comprehensive collections in all subjects up to the current state of knowledge in each, including almost anything of potential value to research. It is now commonly accepted that such completeness is unattainable for a single library (only the Library of Congress comes close to having such an aspiration) and that cooperation among libraries is essential to provide scholars and others with the products of the "knowledge explosion" of the past few decades.

Worldwide, the production of new books has more than doubled in the last twenty years; in the United States alone, the number of books published rose from 15,000 in 1960 to over 45,000 in 1979.[1] The number of scientific and technical books published each year in the United States rose from 3,000 in 1960 to 15,000 in 1980. The number of scientific and technical serial titles, worldwide, rose from less than 20,000 to over 50,000 in the same period.[2]

The explosion of available information not only is fueled by the increases in new knowledge but also provides the base for new research and has changed the methods of research in most fields. Research in the physical and biological sciences depends on almost immediate access to the results of other research everywhere in the world. That access is made possible by the development of on-line computer data bases, abstracts, and other searching tools. The social sciences are increasingly dependent on such techniques as well; most social science disciplines are now focused much more than in the past on analyses of hard data about current phenomena rather than on historical studies. Even in the humanities there is movement toward an emphasis on contemporary issues, on international interests, and on the use of social science techniques in the study of history and literature. These developments have changed the ways in which scholars use the library. Most scholars now require access to a much larger range of materials than any single library can provide in its own collection; therefore, they need more assistance from profes-

---

[1] *The Bowker Annual of Library and Book Trade Information* (New York: R. R. Bowker Co.), p. 327. The number cited does not include U.S. or state government publications or reports, nor doctoral theses.

[2] D. W. King et al., *Statistical Indicators of Scientific and Technical Communication, 1960–1980*, Vol. 1: *A Summary Report for the National Science Foundation, Division of Science Information* (Rockville, Md.: King Research, Inc., Center for Quantitative Sciences, 1976), p. 7. The 1960–1974 figures are from R. R. Bowker Company; 1980 figures are projected by King Research, Inc. The figure for scientific and technical serials includes trade journals and other periodicals not considered to be scholarly scientific and technical literature. Scholarly journals published in the United States probably number over twenty-one hundred.

sional library staff in identifying sources, in sorting out what is relevant, and in locating materials.

Probably the most important technological development for increasing access to materials has been the computerization of bibliographic information for both serials and monographs. The Library of Congress, which has provided cataloguing information for the nation's libraries since 1901, now provides machine-readable bibliographic records for its own acquisitions and uses cataloguing information from several other major research libraries, including the national libraries of several foreign countries. In 1971 OCLC, Inc. (formerly the Ohio College Library Center) began the first successful on-line "bibliographic utility," providing a means of sharing computerized catalogue records produced by the Library of Congress and other contributing libraries. Other organizations now offering similar services include the Research Libraries Group (RLG), whose bibliographic utility is called the Research Libraries Information Network (RLIN), the University of Toronto Library Automation Systems (UTLAS), and the Washington Library Network (WLN). The on-line union catalogues resulting from these services contain information on recently acquired holdings of contributors; borrowing libraries can identify book locations in the data base and, in the case of OCLC and RLG, can transmit loan requests by computer. Recent agreements among several of these utilities to share their data bases will further increase the range of their services to users. Commercial vendors started offering on-line bibliographic search services in the early 1970s; these bring to the attention of users citations to a wide variety of publications, especially in the periodical literature and technical reports.

While bibliographic access has improved, slow delivery of requested items has been a major problem. Research and development work on new techniques of information storage may in the future permit faster location, and new telecommunications techniques may enable information to be transmitted in minutes or seconds.

These technologies will allow a degree of shared access never before possible. Increasingly, bibliographic searches are becoming independent of individual libraries. Eventually, the separate collections of libraries may be viewed as a single large distributed collection to which users can gain quick and efficient access by way of on-line searching and the rapid electronic delivery of items to libraries or offices. In addition, the nation's libraries may enter into more effective and efficient modes of cooperation in developing their collections and in preserving them in order to assure the widest possible access to all materials for their users.

Such a system will require changes in the expectations of scholars about their institution's collections and services and in the ways they use the library. Library directors will need to increase consultation with faculty about collection development and access policies, and faculty must increasingly consult librarians about their curriculum and research plans. In addition, presidents and deans must help faculty to understand and accept new limits on institutional collections and alternative methods for gaining access to needed research materials.

The impetus for sharing resources comes not only from the increases in the amount of material which scholars need and produce, and from the technology that makes sharing possible, but also from sheer economic necessity. American research universities spent over $500 million in 1979–1980 to support the operating expenses of their research libraries. Twenty-four university libraries spent over $7 million each. Inflation has reduced the power of the university budget to buy the goods and services needed; it has hit research libraries even harder than other units. The price of hardcover books more than doubled between 1970 and 1980, and periodical prices have risen 13 percent a year, or a total of 239 percent over the last ten years. The prices for foreign publications have skyrocketed, not only because of inflation but also because of the declining value of the dollar in foreign markets. While expenditures of research libraries for library materials increased by 91 percent between 1970 and 1980, the gross number of volumes added each year *diminished* by 22.5 percent. Library staff salaries have risen as well; the new technology may relieve staff of some repetitive tasks, but it increases the need for specialized skills and services. Although technology may increase the possibilities for sharing, it is expensive; for instance, installation and support costs of the initial links to the RLG data base are expected to exceed $25,000 for each library. Computer video terminals cost $2,500 to $4,000 each. Microforms and optical recording offer technical capability for saving collections threatened by physical deterioration, but capital and operating costs for the foreseeable future are enormous.

Federal regulations requiring access for the handicapped, Occupational Safety and Health Administration (OSHA) regulations, the paperwork involved in affirmative action, indirect cost accounting, and other regulations have also increased library costs.

A major challenge faced by all libraries, but especially by the research libraries with their large retrospective collections, is the preservation of the collection materials needed by future students and scholars. Books and journals printed since about 1850 are, quite literally, falling apart because the paper on which they are printed has too high an acid content. The acid promotes deterioration, especially at high temperatures and improper humidity. This constitutes a national problem of enormous magnitude, which must be solved by coordinated action to avoid the risk of allowing useful publications to crumble into oblivion. A coordinated national policy and strategy, including efforts by each research library, are urgently needed.

Buildings housing many research collections are cramped for space and also are outmoded. The average research library collection has doubled in size every fifteen or twenty years; additional shelf and storage space must be provided. Environmental controls are crucial; air conditioning of storage space would contribute more than any other method to the preservation of collections. Many older buildings, however, are difficult and expensive to adapt to air conditioning; some do not have adequate under-floor and between-wall space to allow for the installation of air conditioning ducts, computer cables, and all the other requirements of modern technology. Because of tight university budgets, most libraries have deferred renovation and maintenance of their buildings, creating problems for the future.

Effective management of modern research libraries requires new kinds of skills and training for library professionals. The research library director and staff are engulfed by new technical and economic realities and many complicated intellectual and political issues. They must be educators of faculty and students in the use of new research techniques, negotiators with the providers of technical and bibliographic services, budget and personnel managers, and long-range planners and policy developers. It is essential that the research library profession be able to attract its share of the brightest people and to offer them the kinds of training required to prepare them to assume these responsibilities. It is equally essential to ensure continued opportunities for professional growth and for appropriate participation in university policy decisions and adequate financial rewards to keep the best people in the profession.

The nation's great research libraries are called on to provide increased levels of service to students, faculty, researchers, business and industry, and other libraries while at the same time trying to cope with the major problems of inflation, adaptation to new technology, physical deterioration of their collections and facilities, and increasing pressures on their budgets. The recommendations which follow attempt to address some of the needs for planning and sharing on a national level and for funding some of the major transformations in research libraries that will enable them to continue serving the nation's scholars in the most effective ways.

A RESEARCH LIBRARIES COUNCIL

The development of recommendations for policy and planning for change on a national basis will require the participation of both users and providers of research library services. Scholars must contribute their advice about the effects on scholarship and research of shared collection policies and new technologies for bibliographic searches; university presidents and chief academic officers must consider the impact of alternative policies on institutional budgets and must be aware that what were once solely library decisions must now become institutional decisions for regional and national involvements; and research librarians must contribute their expertise about the practical—and political—feasibility of policy suggestions.

☐ A new mechanism is required for the setting of national policies and priorities for research libraries. Existing groups concerned with the health of research libraries are either too limited in their membership (such as the Association of Research Libraries, composed of the directors of research libraries) or too broad in their mandate (such as the American Library Association or the National Commission on Libraries and Information Science) to offer both the necessary contributions of scholars and university heads and a concentrated focus on major research libraries. We therefore recommend the establishment of a new Research Libraries Council. This body should be established in such a way that its recommendations are accepted as legitimate both by the providers of library services and by the users of those services. Such a group should be able to recommend to institutions and to libraries methods by which decisions can be made to divide responsibility for providing access to research materials to all scholars. It should be able to speak on behalf of those users and providers to the Congress and to federal agencies. The council should recommend to funding agencies, both private and governmental, priorities for projects which will affect the whole system of research libraries in the United States. It should consult with, and be consulted by, those federal agencies with programs touching on the concerns of research libraries: the National Endowment for the Humanities, the National Science Foundation, and the Office of Libraries and Learning Technologies of the Department of Education. It should provide information and advice to members and staff of congressional committees concerned with legislation affecting research libraries, although direct lobbying efforts should be left to individual associations, institutions, and individuals. The council should enlist the participation of the Library of Congress and of the national libraries in its efforts. It should consult with business and industry and with publishers and secondary publishers and other agencies of the information industry, as well as with other elements of the library community.

The council, in order to be effective, must have continuity of sponsorship and a locus of responsibility for its maintenance and staffing, and yet it should not be seen as the creature of any one of the groups whose interests it serves. The sponsoring group or groups should solicit nominations for membership on the Research Libraries Council from the scholarly societies, from the Association of Research Libraries, and from the Association of American Universities and the National Association of State Universities and Land-Grant Colleges. The direct expenses (for example, travel) of the council might be supported by the individual associations or institutions whose representatives serve on the council; support for staff and office expenses could be sought from foundations and corporations.

WORKING WITH SCHOLARS

☐ Because research libraries are changing so rapidly in response to budgetary constraints and new technological and other opportunities, it is imperative that librarians, scholars, and administrators work together to set policies and priorities for the library and to coordinate curricular and library programs. On each campus, there must be a core of people willing to become knowledgeable about the challenges and opportunities facing the library and to explain them to the faculty at large. Scholars must work with librarians to ensure that librarians are informed about projected needs for library support for teaching and research. Universities should reexamine their mechanisms for ensuring that such exchanges take place and should take whatever steps are needed to improve the communication and policymaking process.

On the national level, while the Research Libraries Council is expected to bring together a group of scholars, administrators, and librarians to identify priorities and to develop policy guidelines to assist research libraries, larger numbers of scholars and administrators should be involved in efforts to understand the problems and to make recommendations for policy. Several useful steps in this direction have been taken recently. One is the establishment, on the recommendation of the National Enquiry into Scholarly Communication,[3] of a standing committee of scholars, publishers, and librarians charged to monitor technological change in the system of scholarly communication. The committee includes members from the American Council of Learned Societies, the Association of Research Libraries, and the American Association of University Presses. The National Enquiry also recommended that the National Endowment for the Humanities establish an office of scholarly communication for the same purpose.[4] We support that recommendation.

The Association of American Universities, the Council on Library Resources, and the Association of Research Libraries have recently established a group of task forces to examine research library issues. They are planning several conferences among librarians, scholars, and university administrators to inform scholars and administrators about library challenges, to clarify the issues and choices which face each university in dealing with them, and to work on the development of policies for obtaining understanding and assistance from the private sector as well as from the government. These timely initiatives need the support of all parts of the university.

☐ The establishment by the Association of American Universities and the Association of Research Libraries of a

---

[3] *Scholarly Communication: The Report of the National Enquiry* (Baltimore: The Johns Hopkins University Press, 1979), p. 29.
[4] Ibid., p. 28.

joint standing committee of research library directors, university presidents, and university chief academic officers to monitor needs and developments in library–scholarly communication would also be useful. Such a group might also develop new models of procedures to enhance such communication on individual campuses.

CENTERS OF SPECIAL RESPONSIBILITY

We have noted above that no library can expect to be self-sufficient in meeting all the needs of its patrons in every conceivable field. The proliferation of scholarly books and journals and their increased costs have made that economically unfeasible. At the same time, advances in bibliographic services, automated data bases, and abstracting and indexing services have increased the knowledge of scholars about existing sources of information and therefore increased their demands for access to those sources. In addition, not only are libraries running out of storage space, but retrospective collections are increasingly threatened by physical deterioration because of the use of acidic paper in book and journal production during the past century and because of continuing adverse environmental conditions.

All of these factors argue for increased cooperation among libraries in meeting the needs of their users, particularly for materials which are not frequently used. It is inefficient for fifty or a hundred libraries to acquire, catalogue, and try to preserve and store materials which may be requested as seldom as once every five or ten years after the first year. What is needed is the assurance that at least one copy will be available when needed and that it can be provided without undue delay.

Two kinds of solutions to these questions are possible. One is the establishment of centralized collections dedicated to lending, such as the National Library of Medicine or the Center for Research Libraries. The National Library of Medicine is a federally supported collection; the center's collection is supported by its members, who agree to contribute materials for storage and lending and to fund the central acquisition of expensive, infrequently used materials which can be borrowed by any member library. These centralized collections are an important supplement to other methods.

The other solution is the sharing of responsibility for collection and preservation in certain fields among groups of libraries. One promising example among research libraries is the emerging Collection Development Program of the Research Libraries Group (RLG), whose twenty-five members are negotiating agreements for assigning to individual libraries collection and preservation responsibilities in particular areas, thus giving the other members the option not to collect in those areas. To a limited extent, the support of special collections, such as those of the area studies centers funded in part by Title VI of the National Defense Education Act, serves the same purpose.

Because programs such as these require long-term commitments to acquire and preserve certain materials and because they also require considerable financial investments, agreements must be voluntary and must be negotiated by a process which involves not only library directors and staff but also the faculty and administration of the institutions involved. Attempts to extend such agreements broadly on a regional and national basis could be assisted by the Research Libraries Council working with its constituents to help to establish priorities and to expedite the process of implementation in cooperation with other interested groups.

☐ The research universities and nonuniversity research library boards should establish, on a voluntary basis, such a system of Centers of Special Responsibility through which responsibility for the acquisition, maintenance, and preservation of regional or national collections in particular topics or areas and responsibility for creating and maintaining the related data bases and for providing access to the collections might be divided among the libraries.

Agreements to distribute responsibility for collection and preservation in particular fields could result in significant savings for libraries as a group, but the individual participants will need additional funds to bring such a system into being. Funding will be required for the maintenance and expansion of collections in the areas of special responsibility and for preservation projects such as mass de-acidification of paper and microfilming or digital or video storage. Funds will also be needed to develop and to put into place the new technology which will be required to ensure access to these collections for all scholars in terms of the new storage and delivery systems noted in the section below on technology.

If the libraries, with the concurrence of their constituents, can agree among themselves on the distribution of responsibilities for collection and preservation and the provision of access, then federal funding should be made available to help them carry out those responsibilities. Title II C of the Higher Education Act was originally conceived of as supporting such a purpose. However, it has never been funded at more than $6 million, and the regulations under the title have not in the past encouraged the possibility of such planning on a national basis. If the funding were increased to the $10 million for FY 1982 and the $15 million for subsequent years now authorized,[5] and if requirements for commitments to special collections and services were mandated, considerable progress could be made in the development of the Centers of Special Responsibility.

A NATIONAL PERIODICALS CENTER

While the National Library of Medicine and the National Agriculture Library serve as limited-purpose national libraries, the United States lacks the kind of national library

---

[5]The original 1976 authorization for Part C of Title II of the Higher Education Act was $20 million; this was reduced to $15 million in the 1980 reauthorization. Numerous groups of scholars have recommended full funding of Title II C at the $20 million level, among them the Commission on the Humanities (*The Humanities in American Life* [Berkeley: University of California Press, 1980], p. 98), the Carnegie Council on Policy Studies in Higher Education (*Three Thousand Futures: The Next Twenty Years for Higher Education* [San Francisco: Jossey-Bass, Inc.,

and national library system established by the British and the French. For a number of years librarians hoped that the Library of Congress could serve as a national library, with both general service and lending responsibilities, and that it might, in particular, develop a program of lending periodicals. That plan failed to materialize, but the possibility of establishing an alternative national lending library has attracted wide support among research librarians and university administrators.

The most recent serious effort to establish the beginnings of a national lending library has been the introduction of legislation to establish a National Periodicals Center (NPC), with the aim of improving access to periodicals for all users in the nation. It is envisaged that the NPC would establish a basic collection of 30,000–60,000 periodicals dedicated to making copies available to libraries and their patrons. The existence of the NPC collection would assure access to periodicals to which the user's library did not subscribe or which were not on its shelves when needed. An important function of the NPC would be the preservation of the retrospective collection. Cost savings to libraries are expected to come primarily from savings in binding and storage costs rather than from cancellation of subscriptions since libraries will continue to subscribe to those journals which are regularly required by their own users. The NPC would be the core of a broader National Periodicals System; it would contract with libraries and commercial sources which chose to cooperate with the system to provide copies of periodicals not held by the center.

Because of incomplete understanding on the part of some scholars and the publishers of small scholarly journals and in the information industry, the NPC authorizing legislation was reduced to authorization for further study of a National Periodical System by a board to be appointed by the president.

1980], p. 127), and the National Enquiry into Scholarly Communication (*Scholarly Communication*, p. 18).

☐ Supporters of the NPC, which include fifteen library, professional, and higher education associations, believe that no further study is needed to establish the desirability or feasibility of an NPC, although clearly an implementation plan will be required before the center begins operations. However, the current legislation offers a good beginning, and its provisions should be funded.[6]

☐ As an interim measure, an initial phase or several phases of a national periodicals center should be established on a private basis. The Center for Research Libraries has the expertise and plans to acquire adequate space to begin such a project in a specific area such as scientific or foreign journals if sufficient funding can be found. The center is working with the Association of Research Libraries to develop such a plan. While this should be regarded as a permanent project, it would also serve to demonstrate the techniques and effects of an NPC as part of the broader National Periodicals System to be established under federal legislation and with federal support. It deserves private foundation and corporate financial support and commitments by university and other research libraries to support and use it.

Further financial support for this undertaking could come through the cooperative efforts of a number of research libraries to develop related projects for funding through Title II C funds.

PRESERVATION

The serious national problem posed by the rapid deterioration of library and archival materials has been mentioned

---

[6]Like the proposal for full funding for Title II C of the Higher Education Act, proposals for a national periodicals center have received wide support from the higher education community and from scholarly associations and commissions. Among the supporters are the Association of American Universities, the National Enquiry into Scholarly Communication (*Scholarly Communication*, p. 19), the Commission on the Humanities (*The Humanities in American Life*, p. 97), and the Carnegie Council on Policy Studies in Higher Education (*Three Thousand Futures*, p. 127).

above. Millions of volumes of printed materials and non-print materials such as manuscripts, maps, and photographs are endangered. Although the efforts of individual libraries and of the Centers of Special Responsibility and the National Periodicals Center proposed above will make a beginning in addressing this challenge, an overall national plan which would address the preservation problem for all important collections, wherever located, is urgently needed.

Such a national plan might combine the preservation responsibilities of a number of individual libraries with regional or national storage facilities for preservation copies of items essential for research, available for reproduction on demand. Microform or video disc production and distribution could be part of the system. It would require a bibliographic mechanism to inform all libraries of what has been safely stored and fast reliable delivery systems for providing access to stored information. And it will require cooperation from publishers to ensure that the problem is not perpetuated through the continued use of acid paper.

☐ The formulation of a national program of preservation will require some kind of coordinating body to recommend policies and priorities and to oversee the negotiation of agreements with individual institutions and groups. It will also require considerable funding both from the institutions themselves and from private foundations and the federal government. The Research Libraries Council should undertake the responsibility for identifying or establishing an appropriate body to develop national policies for the preservation of library and archival materials and to recommend funding mechanisms for implementation of those policies.

☐ The National Endowment for the Humanities (NEH) has established a program of incentive grants for institutions to undertake planning and projects in preservation. Its staff have established good relationships not only with individual libraries and library associations but also with groups such as the National Historical Publications and Records Commission, the National Conservation Advisory Council, and publishers. The Endowment should build on this background of linkages between the scholarly world, publishing, and research libraries and continue its preservation programs.

RESEARCH NEEDS

Profound changes are now underway and more are anticipated both in the way in which research libraries operate internally and in the ways they work together as they seek to improve their support of research and instruction. These changes and changes in the nature of scholarship itself will in turn alter the ways in which scholars and students use the library. If libraries are to fulfill their obligations responsibly so that changes are positive rather than disruptive, we need to understand much more thoroughly than we now do the ways in which research libraries actually operate, how information is organized and used, and what the effects of various alternative policies might be on the behavior of users and the satisfaction of their needs.

There is wide agreement that current collection of data and levels of analysis and planning are not adequate to inform the fundamental decisions which must now be made both about individual libraries and about research library services on a national level. There is a need for a structured and purposefully organized program of research and evaluation to address key issues facing research libraries.

Several approaches to meeting research needs are possible. The Council on Library Resources is now planning an annual invitational conference on the "Frontiers of Librarianship," which will "seek to establish the context—intellectual, economic, technical, and political—in which research libraries are likely to be operating through the end of this century and to identify the tests against which library performance will, in the long term, be measured."[7]

---

[7]Personal communication from W. J. Haas to B. Turlington, June 1980.

Fundamental questions about the relationship of research libraries to scholarship and scholarly communication will be emphasized. The council hopes to link a new research effort to these conferences, with commissioned papers laying out the issues and with funded research on particular topics growing out of the discussions.

☐ The Association of Research Libraries and the Research Libraries Council are also appropriate bodies to help to set the agenda and priorities for research. They should work with the Council on Library Resources, library schools, library directors, scholars, and others concerned with the health of research libraries to establish a research agenda for the next decade and to engage in needed data collection and analysis. Funds are potentially available through Title II B of the Higher Education Act, through the Division of Information Science and Technology of the National Science Foundation, and through private and corporate foundations.

TECHNOLOGY

As noted in the introduction to this chapter, research libraries are entering a period of major revolution in the way they provide services to their users. As bibliographical tools become nationwide and worldwide rather than specific to a particular collection, students and scholars demand access to an ever-wider pool of research materials at the same time that individual libraries are less able to provide these materials in their own collections. New technologies, some now in existence and some still being developed, will be needed to provide this access.

The application of new technologies has already had a substantial impact on the operations of research libraries. Computers are widely used for cataloguing and circulation records and are beginning to have an effect on serials control, acquisitions, and resource sharing. The use of microforms has grown rapidly, with the ratio of printed volumes to microforms in libraries of the Association of Research

Libraries changing from 3 to 1 in 1973 to 1.8 to 1 in 1979.[8] In the future, digital storage and video discs will be used increasingly for preservation and storage of materials.

Progress in the reproduction and transmission of copies of documents has been less rapid. (One of the reasons that microfilm has never been very popular with users is that the microform readers have never matched the technical advances of the film.) But new developments are on the horizon, with work now underway, for example, on rapid scanning and transmission of printed information in lieu of photocopying for interlibrary lending.

No revolution of this order of magnitude has occurred before in the history of libraries. As was pointed out in *Research Universities and the National Interest*, "A remarkable opportunity exists to extend the role of libraries and thus the ultimate impact of research and scholarship."[9] As the transition to new technology takes place, it is important to emphasize that fact. Research libraries exist to serve scholarship and teaching—scholars and students. The only meaningful test of proposals to improve libraries is the extent to which they serve those purposes. Perhaps the greatest enemy of the constructive application of new technology to the service of scholarship would be undiscriminating enthusiasm. Thoughtful advocates of technological solutions to research library problems will recognize that the very cost of those solutions places on their advocates the burden to prove that they will provide better results than more conventional methods. The apparently dazzling prospects held out by the new technologies can overwhelm prudent judgment and lead to large and costly errors. The problems of libraries are real; efforts to solve them must be accompanied by dispassionate evaluation, lest the efforts themselves create even larger problems.

The new technology is expensive, with high costs for

[8] Association of Research Libraries, *ARL Statistics, 1979* (Washington, D.C.: Association of Research Libraries, 1980).

[9] *Research Universities and the National Interest: A Report from Fifteen University Presidents* (New York: The Ford Foundation, 1978), pp. 91–92.

the purchase and maintenance of equipment and for the conversion of physical facilities to accommodate computers, video disc players, and so forth. In addition, during a period of transition—from card catalogues to on-line computer catalogues, for instance—there will be costs for operating two systems simultaneously. While computerized operations have freed some staff time from repetitive tasks, allowing more time for direct services to users, in general the use of new technologies in research libraries has so far tended to be incremental rather than displacive in terms of overall operations. If further advances are to be made, it will be important to select those applications where the growth of such factors as staff, budget, and collection might be slowed and, at the same time, the quality and level of service might be enhanced. Improved document delivery systems allowing more rational collection development policies are but one example.

It is most unlikely that the universities, with their restricted budgets, will be able to shoulder alone the financial burdens of the transition to a new technology. While continuing investments will be needed, it is clear that many of the conversion and capital costs will be one-time expenses, and it is in this area that major help will be needed. Several existing federal programs might provide support. Title II C funds could be used to make possible the use of new technologies for the electronic communication of materials to improve access through interlibrary loan, for example. Title III of the Library Services and Construction Act, which supports networking efforts by grants to states, might be used to fund computers and telecommunications devices. Title VII of the Higher Education Act, especially if it is adequately funded, should support the renovation of library facilities where needed to accommodate the new technology and can also be used for the purchase of major equipment. Research facilities and equipment grants through the National Science Foundation and other agencies could be helpful. National Endowment for the Humanities grants have been made for a number of preservation projects and could support the development and dissemination of new technology in that area.

☐ Private foundations have already given generous support to some new technological uses. Corporations and corporate foundations might find technology a particularly appropriate field for their support of research libraries. Both monetary support and support in the area of technical advice and training would be helpful, as would direct grants of equipment.

☐ The federal government, state governments, foundations, and corporations should mount a special ten-year project for funding the transition to a new technology for research libraries. Coordination could be provided by the Research Libraries Council working with its constituent groups.

THE ROLE OF THE PRIVATE SECTOR— CORPORATE SUPPORT

Research libraries support research not only in the academic community but also in business and industry. A number of corporations are quite explicit about the extent to which they depend on the collections of research libraries in their area; many have planned the location of their businesses with nearby library facilities in mind. Many industries maintain their own special libraries, but they tend to be limited to current materials; the maintenance of large retrospective collections is simply too expensive to be practical, given their limited use.

☐ Some corporations are critical of the limitations which research libraries have imposed on corporate use of their collections. Although many research libraries have worked out agreements with nearby corporations for corporate payment of fees for library services, these are not universal, especially where the library's facilities are already strained by services to students and scholars. While this situation may be ameliorated in the future by technological developments which improve interlibrary loan and permit the electronic transmission of materials, that will take time. In the meantime, it would be useful to both corporations and research libraries to have more information about existing successful arrangements. The Association of Research Libraries should collect such information and should consider the development of model agreements which might be used by those libraries and corporations desiring closer cooperative ties.

Industry and business contribute over $750 million a year to American higher education, 80 percent in the form of research grants, capital grants, and grants for other special purposes. Although such support has been growing over the past decade, corporations are not generally aware of research library issues. The recent distribution by the Carnegie Corporation of a brochure describing research library needs should be useful in this regard. Further giving might also be stimulated by the presentation by universities of particular projects for funding for their research libraries.

☐ Corporations should increase their giving to individual research libraries and should also be encouraged to give to group library projects in addition to their normal giving to individual universities. The Council on Library Resources and the Research Libraries Council proposed above could develop or identify specific proposals for system-wide projects which might be appropriate for corporate support. Examples include support for purchase of equipment and new developmental work at the Center for Research Libraries and/or a National Periodicals Center, support of specialized central collections of particular interest to industry and business, support for the equipment and research necessary for linking the data bases of the major bibliographic utilities, support for research and development of technology for rapid computer scanning and transmission of materials for interlibrary loan, and support of various group efforts to build cooperative collection development and preservation systems.

☐ In addition to monetary support, a number of corporations might be in a position to offer substantial technical assistance to research libraries in the area of communications technology. Universities might establish corporate advisory committees for their libraries to assist in selecting and establishing the most efficient and effective information technology systems. The universities should find ways of directing more corporate attention to the needs both of individual research libraries and of cooperative projects to increase services to users.

☐ The Association of Research Libraries could usefully collect and disseminate information about existing corporate/research library cooperative agreements and should consider developing a model agreement for those who would like to increase such cooperation.

THE ROLE OF THE RESEARCH LIBRARIAN

Our final recommendation is addressed to university heads and to the boards of nonuniversity research libraries. It is a plea for recognition of the importance of the research librarian to the health of the research enterprise. The complexity of the tasks of developing policies for and of managing the operations of the research library and of presiding over the major transformations that will take place in research libraries over the next decades demands the leadership of the very best people. If not enough highly skilled people are attracted into the profession, research and teaching will suffer.

The major research libraries of the future will require specialized professional staff of the highest quality, including subject specialists, computer and communications experts, and well-trained financial and other administrators. Library training programs must become more sophisticated and more interdisciplinary. New programs will be needed to retrain library personnel to handle effectively the new responsibilities of the research library and the reorganization of the structure of the library that will be needed to meet those responsibilities. Librarians must be able to work with faculty on curricular policy as well as on the support of research. University administrators must recognize that the best people will not be attracted to or remain in the profession unless they are included in policymaking and are paid salaries equivalent to other professional salaries. It is difficult to imagine that a fair share of the best young people will be attracted to a profession that still, in 1982, pays beginning salaries of $12,000 and relatively low salaries to all but the highest level of professionals.

☐ A number of efforts are now under way, through the Council on Library Resources and the Association of Research Libraries, to strengthen programs for the training of research librarians. Those efforts must be matched by the willingness of universities and library boards to recognize and to increase the significant policy and management roles played by their professional librarians in the support of teaching and research and to reward their best people appropriately. Sufficient resources must be invested in professional library staffs to attract and keep people of the highest intellectual and managerial capabilities.

CHAPTER FIVE

THE ERODING RESEARCH BASE:
Facilities and Instrumentation

The conduct of scientific research at the frontiers of knowledge and the training of advanced students require not only highly qualified investigators and teachers but also increasingly sophisticated—and expensive—research instrumentation and facilities. Several recent studies have documented a severe threat to the quality of scientific research and advanced training due to a serious deterioration in the quality of the tools necessary for the research and of the facilities where the research is done. Dr. George A. Keyworth, the president's science advisor, at his Senate confirmation hearings in July 1981 described the current status of university research facilities as "disgraceful and deplorable" and noted that the situation offers "unattractive prospects" for those interested in pursuing careers in experimental science.

A study of research instrumentation conducted by the Association of American Universities (AAU) for the National Science Foundation in 1980 found that the median age of research instrumentation in many leading university

This paper is based on studies conducted by the Association of American Universities in 1980 and 1981 and on a 1979 survey and proposal for new funding initiatives for research facilities by Robert K. Durkee of Princeton University.

laboratories is now twice that of the instrumentation in leading commercial laboratories.[1] The scientific equipment available to American researchers is probably already inferior to that found in laboratories in Western Europe and Japan, both in quantity and in quality. There is mounting evidence that foreign laboratories are surpassing the capacity of American ones to do state-of-the-art research.

A survey of the research facilities needs of leading universities completed by the AAU in the spring of 1981[2] has shown that many of the nation's leading university research laboratories are in serious disrepair; major renovation and repairs are needed to update laboratories constructed in the 1960s and before, and new construction is needed to provide facilities adequate for research which requires the latest instrumentation and methodologies. This does not mean that these universities have not been investing in research facilities; the fifteen institutions included in the AAU survey reported that they had spent $400 million in the last four years for new construction, facility modernization, major repair and renovation, and special purpose research equipment in five scientific areas and in medical schools at ten of the institutions. But they estimate that they would need more than $765 million over the next three years merely to upgrade their facilities to allow faculty now in place to carry out their research.

REASONS FOR THE DECLINE

Increased Costs of Modern Equipment

A number of factors have contributed to the decline of the quality of research facilities and instrumentation during the past decade. The first is that the costs of instrumentation and facilities have increased at exceedingly rapid rates not

---

[1] Association of American Universities, *The Scientific Instrumentation Needs of Research Universities: A Report to the National Science Foundation* (Washington, D.C., 1980).

[2] Association of American Universities, *The Nation's Deteriorating University Research Facilities: A Survey of Recent Expenditures and Projected Needs in Fifteen Universities* (Washington, D.C., 1981).

only because of inflation but also because the technological advances which have dramatically increased the precision, capacity, and speed of today's instruments have also dramatically increased their costs.

These advances have redefined research frontiers and opened new horizons. But they have also rendered obsolete equipment purchased only a few years before. Data gathered by the National Science Foundation indicate that the costs of equipping laboratories in various scientific fields increased at annual rates ranging from 13 percent to 23 percent between 1970 and 1978. The AAU instrumentation study showed that the start-up laboratory instrumentation needed for a new faculty member in synthetic organic chemistry, which cost $8,000 in 1970, by 1979 cost $43,850—an increase of 550 percent in nine years. Costs of the departmental equipment to which such a researcher requires access rose from $116,600 in 1970 to $741,000 in 1979, a 636 percent increase. An unpublished 1979 study by the National Bureau of Standards found that a basic microanalytical chemistry laboratory that would have required some $10,000 worth of heavy instrumentation in 1960 now would require more than $1 million to equip to modern standards.

Declining Federal Support

While costs have been climbing, the availability of funds for instrumentation and facilities has been declining. In particular, the federal funding that was available to construct facilities and to buy major equipment in a time of rapid expansion of federal investment in basic research has steadily eroded. In 1965 the federal government provided about $126 million for research facilities on university and college campuses; by 1979 that figure had shrunk to about $32 million.[3]

---

[3]Those figures are in current dollars. In constant 1972 dollars the decline is, of course, much more dramatic, from $212.2 million to $22.4 million.

Federal funds are still available for research facilities, but a very small proportion goes to university laboratories. The National Science Foundation's *Science Indicators* published in 1979 reported that over three-fourths of all federal support for R&D plant is now being allocated to federal intramural laboratories and industry.[4] In 1977, the most recent year for which figures were available, less than 2.5 percent of such funds went to colleges and universities. Moreover, the ratio of federal funds for R&D plant to total federal support for R&D at colleges and universities decreased steadily from 11 percent in 1966 to 1 percent in 1977.

For instrumentation and equipment, the primary source of funding for university laboratories is federal research grants; almost 60 percent of equipment funds in private universities and nearly 50 percent in public universities come from such grants. Between 1968 and 1978, the proportion of the nation's gross national product spent on basic research declined from .27 percent to .20 percent; the decline in federal investment in basic research at colleges and universities during that period was about 5 percent when adjusted for the overall rate of inflation.

Not only has there been a decline in federal funding for basic research, but also there was a decline in the percentage of project support going to equipment during the decade from the mid-sixties to the mid-seventies. The major sources of equipment support are the National Science Foundation and the National Institutes of Health (NIH), which together provide about two-thirds of all federal grant funds to colleges and universities to support scientific research. At NSF, the percentage of project support going to permanent equipment declined from 11.2 percent in 1966 to 5.4 percent in 1974; by 1978 it was back up to 13 percent (including funding for instrumentation centers

[4]National Science Board, National Science Foundation, *Science Indicators 1978: Report of the National Science Board 1979* (Washington, D.C., 1979).

and teaching instrumentation). At NIH, expenditures for equipment declined from 11.4 percent of total funding in 1966 to 5.7 percent in 1974 and 5.5 percent in 1977.

The National Institutes of Health provide Biomedical Research Support Grants (BRSGs) for the general support of research and research training programs. These grants, which are awarded in relationship to the size of the research grant programs of the participating institutions, make available flexible discretionary funds to strengthen the research capabilities of institutions doing biomedical research under NIH grants. About 30 percent of the grants has been used for equipment purchases, with the rest going mostly to salary support of new investigators, students, and technical/research assistants and to other direct costs of supporting research. In 1969, BRSGs were funded at a level of 8.3 percent of NIH research project grants. The percentage has been declining ever since; it was down to 2.2 percent in FY 1980. The amount of individual grants has declined 6.2 percent in actual dollars and 25.8 percent in real dollars since 1976, with an even larger impact on the grantees doing the most research.

The National Science Foundation administered a similar program—the Institutional Improvement for Science Program—from 1961 to 1974. During those years over 50 percent of the funds were used to acquire instrumentation.[5]

Operation and Maintenance Costs

Meeting the costs required to operate and maintain their research instrumentation is an almost universal problem among the major research universities. Operation and maintenance costs cover a variety of expenses, including service contracts for commercial instruments, replacement parts, the cost of staff salaries and equipment for support shops, and the expense of simply operating the instruments. Equipment such as large computers often requires

---

[5]J. G. Danek, "Institutional Management and Utilization of National Science Foundation Institutional Grants for Science," *Dissertation Abstracts International* 38 (Ann Arbor, Mich.: University Microfilms, 1976), 181.

the installation of special air conditioning facilities. Some instruments require hiring a full-time operator. When departments cannot adequately meet these costs, instruments may be inadequately maintained, shortening their useful life; without sufficient support personnel, projects are delayed, and faculty and students must function as technicians, with a consequent loss of research and training time.

The costs of service contracts have increased substantially over the last few years and represent a major financial burden to many departments. In one molecular biology laboratory which relies heavily on centrifugation, the average cost of service contracts on centrifuges increased almost 100 percent between 1975 and 1979. Laboratory equipment also needs expert maintenance on the campus. For example, much of the instrumentation used in physics departments is either built in-house or is commercially manufactured instrumentation that is substantially modified in-house. Such departments therefore require well-equipped machine shops and electronics shops staffed by skilled technicians. When shop support is inadequate, faculty and students are forced to devote research time to operation and maintenance functions.

The operation of many instruments used by individual researchers also generates substantial ongoing expenses. A cryogenic magnetometer, for instance, which cost $30,000 to purchase, requires $8,000 in annual operating expenses, principally for liquid helium. Thus, the yearly operating expenses of this instrument are over one-fourth of the acquisition cost. The plasma tubes for an argon-ion laser must be replaced at an average annual cost of $10,000.

Researchers who are forced to work with outdated instrumentation are confronted with special operation and maintenance problems. Their equipment, by virtue of its age, may be more difficult to operate and is more likely to break down. Moreover, manufacturers may refuse to carry a service contract on an old instrument, or spare parts may no longer be available.

Operation and maintenance costs are a continuing expense, which, if not adequately funded, can cripple a research program. These costs may become one of the greatest problems for research programs in the future.

As with equipment, facilities now more quickly become dated to the point where they can no longer accommodate the demands of modern science. Many older buildings, for instance, do not have adequate plumbing connections to service modern animal care facilities or adequate space for computer wiring. They also, of course, require maintenance and repairs. The costs of normal building repairs (such as new roofs, maintenance of utilities and other services, structural repairs, and minor remodeling) and the routine costs of operation (including energy and janitorial costs) have been increasing at a faster rate than inflation in the economy as a whole. At the same time, many of the leading facilities of the major research universities which were constructed during the expansive 1960s are now beginning to require substantial maintenance and renovation. In many cases, these increased needs must compete for funds not only with other ongoing projects but also with a backlog of maintenance needs deferred under the stringent financial circumstances of the 1970s.

Federal Regulations

The costs of maintaining research facilities have been greatly increased in recent years by an expanded awareness of health and safety aspects of research facilities and equipment. This awareness has led to new requirements for occupational health and safety, new standards for handling dangerous biological materials, and new legal mandates for improvement in such facilities as experimental animal accommodations. Additional recent constraints on the disposition of hazardous wastes have imposed significant increased costs on already hard-pressed research budgets.

Title VII of the Higher Education Act, among other provisions, authorizes grants and loans to institutions of higher education for "the construction, reconstruction, or renovation of academic facilities and the acquisition of special equipment to enable such institutions to bring their academic facilities into conformity with the requirements of

. . . environmental protection or health and safety programs mandated by federal, state, or local law. . . ." The law also authorizes funds to increase energy efficiency and to expand access for the handicapped. While the likelihood of funding for this program at the present time is small, its provisions might be used in the future under more auspicious budgetary circumstances.

CONSEQUENCES OF INADEQUATE FACILITIES AND INSTRUMENTATION

The combined problems of inflation and obsolescence in instrumentation and facilities, along with decreasing federal funding, compound the overall inflationary pressures on university budgets. Even under the most austere budgets, increases in costs are outpacing increases in revenues, and many needed improvements and purchases have had to be postponed. The resulting backlog of equipment and facility needs, coupled with the prospect of continuing inflation and even more stringent institutional budgets, means that important work will not be done or that it will not be done as well or as quickly as it could be done and that theoretical work will be further divorced from the practical, experimental work that both tests and informs theory. As Smith and Karlesky pointed out in 1977: "Over the long run, inability to take advantage of improved instrumentation makes a qualitative as well as a quantitative difference."[6]

Consequences for Science

During the AAU facilities study cited above, leading researchers in all fields expressed a growing conviction that U.S. scientific research and advanced training face serious threats to their quality and productivity because of the obsolescence of our research laboratories and scientific instru-

---

[6]Bruce L. Smith and Joseph J. Karlesky, *The State of Academic Science: The Universities in the Nation's Research Effort* (New York, Change Magazine Press, 1977), p. 168.

mentation. Faculty in leading departments reported that they are unable to work at the cutting edge of their fields. Promising lines of investigation are being foreclosed, and the efficiency of research output is sacrificed. The quality of training provided to advanced graduate students is compromised as programs are forced to shift from costly experimental research and training to more theoretical approaches.

As a result, leading departments are increasingly frustrated in their efforts to attract and hold quality researchers and advanced graduate students because they are unable to offer candidates the modern research environments necessary to conduct competitive research and training programs. Many are unable to retain present faculty, especially in certain engineering fields, because the best faculty are being attracted away by superior industrial, government, and sometimes foreign research laboratories.

Schools of engineering report serious deficiencies in instructional facilities. Research and instruction in important new areas such as computer-aided design and computer-aided manufacturing, fields directly related to future improvements in industrial productivity and innovation, are seriously hampered, thus compromising the nation's ability to meet vigorous foreign competition.

A young biologist at Brown University speculates that because of the inability of his university and others to purchase modern electron microscopes:

> In the next decade, American leadership in cell biology and ultra structural studies will be surrendered to well-equipped laboratories in Europe and Japan. Soon American students of science will find it necessary to study in those places rather than having the best scientists in the world come to these shores to do their work.[7]

A botanist at the University of Maryland says:

---

[7] The quotations in the sections that follow are from the supplement to the Association of American Universities study, *The Nation's Deteriorating University Research Facilities.*

More and more of our faculty have had to turn away from the "cutting edge" of science in the last ten years due to the unavailability of chromatographic equipment, spectrometers and computerized equipment of various kinds. This lack of equipment, labor, and even routine supplies of all kinds have forced a number of our faculty into "descriptive biology" of the 1920s caliber. . . . Our ability to do research at even the 1960 level diminishes each year due to the lack of funds for modernization.

At the University of Wisconsin, a zoologist reports: "The zoology department has declined the opportunity to carry out experiments on certain proven hazardous substances which the National Institutes of Environmental Health Sciences had wanted tested because the department lacks adequate ventilation and chemical hoods for proper fume exhaustion." At UCLA, "Critical work in the area of cell cycle research and hormonal effects on cell cycle is not being done due to the absence of a computer coupled cell sorter."

A chemist at Northwestern University states:

We are attempting 1981 research in a 1941 building and the forty-year gap is too painfully apparent. In the past four years the department's total general research dollars have more than doubled, faculty members have won several national named research awards, and several entirely new research programs have begun. We may, however, now have reached the point at which simple space difficulties very significantly impede our continued progress. The limitations imposed on our research by present facilities . . . mean that several faculty have delayed or avoided starting particular projects because there is no space even to start. This is especially worrisome because the most innovative and promising research is often put off in favor of easier to arrange efforts.

At the University of Utah, a chemist, after reviewing his department's unmet needs for a mass spectrometer and other instrumentation, states: "It is not an exaggeration to say that with proper instrumentation and engineering and technician support, we could tackle problems which we presently only dream about and could probably raise the output of first-class science by a factor of two."

The School of Engineering at Pennsylvania State University reports:

> The inadequate and obsolete equipment that the Civil Engineering Department currently has in some research laboratories is a severe handicap to our faculty and graduate students. The lack of modern equipment eliminates our faculty from bidding on many sponsored projects. Graduate students are handicapped because their theses and dissertations are restricted by the capabilities of our present equipment. The net result is a gradual decrease in the quality of research performed at the University and a deficiency in our education of graduate students.

Medical schools as well as science departments are facing serious limitations because of lack of space and equipment. The Cornell University medical school reports that

> under present circumstances there is virtually no room for the development of new programs in biomedical research. We have no facilities adequate for recombinant DNA studies. We have no storage facility for many hazardous chemicals. About 35 percent of our research laboratories has not been fully modernized since the buildings were built in 1932 . . . it would require about $14 million to completely modernize the laboratories. Ventilation and hood facilities in these laboratories are substandard by present criteria. Also sprinklers and showers have not been installed in most of the laboratories. It is estimated that up to $3 million of the renovation cost could be spent just to meet present safety regulations.

Consequences for Industry

Although industrial laboratories engage in some basic research, in this country most of it is done by university laboratories, much of it under federal grants or contracts and some under industry contracts. These laboratories produce the new knowledge and the base of information from which industry starts its applied research and developmental work. Many leading industrial companies are eager to join with American universities in developing cooperative programs for strengthening the basic understanding of the processes on which they depend so critically, in fields ranging from alternative energy sources to recombinant DNA research.

Industry depends on universities to provide the advanced training in science, technology, management, the social sciences, and other fields to meet corporate manpower needs. If the universities do not have adequate state-of-the-art facilities and instrumentation, they cannot produce trained people to meet industrial needs. This fact was echoed many times by the faculty and researchers questioned during the AAU facilities study. Many reported the sense that their students were being inadequately trained in innovative work with modern instruments of high quality. They are therefore unfamiliar with the potential of these facilities, which limits their contribution to industry. For some, the solution has been to send students to national laboratories or abroad, where new equipment seems more accessible. The fear was repeatedly expressed that not only is the United States losing its competitive edge in the production of new knowledge but that it is also on the verge of handicapping a whole generation of young scientists because of inadequate facilities and instrumentation.

In the area of biomedical research, scientists at both the University of Florida and Brown University report that the biomedical and health products industry is increasingly seeking channels of research operation abroad, especially in Japan and West Germany. Engineers at Northwestern and Stanford report the same for their fields, as do geologists at Cornell and chemists at the University of Florida and the University of Utah.

For instance, engineers report that groups in Japan and France, but not in the United States, can produce ultra-high purity iron, which exhibits properties which are drastically different from those observed in high purity iron commercially. Because of this, the United States will likely miss out on the opportunity to discover and understand the intrinsic properties of iron and steel, an understanding of obvious commercial significance.

A chemist notes that much of the new technology essential for chemistry research is heavily dependent on electronic and optical equipment such as computers and lasers, instruments which are now produced primarily in Japan and Germany.

The October 1980 report to the president by the National Science Foundation and the Department of Education, *Science and Engineering Education for the 1980s and Beyond*, notes that one of the problems in attracting qualified faculty members in engineering and computer fields is inadequate equipment and facilities for research. "An important additional problem in engineering education is a severe lack of the equipment required for instructional purposes at the undergraduate level." Major companies now depend on computer-aided design and computer-assisted manufacturing methods, but "the apparatus to teach these methods to students is generally unavailable in engineering schools. Consequently, a good deal of the instruction being offered may in fact be obsolete."[8] Much the same situation obtains in most schools of business and in other professional and graduate schools.

Consequences to Government

The U.S. government has depended on research conducted in university laboratories for advances in a wide variety of fields, especially in defense, health, agriculture, and energy resources. Many universities report that their work in these fields is now seriously impeded by inadequate facilities and instrumentation. For example, during the AAU study on research facilities, Northwestern University noted that its research in lasers has essentially stopped due to lack of space and electric power. "Work on anti-cancer agents is

---

[8] National Science Foundation and Department of Education, *Science and Engineering Education for the 1980s and Beyond* (Washington, D.C., 1980).

very seriously impeded by the lack of suitable NMR apparatus to help identify the agents when they are prepared. We have lost a faculty member largely because of this shortcoming in facilities."

Biologists at the University of Illinois are heavily involved in research on environmental protection, energy, and food production; while the university is remodeling and upgrading space, it continues to have difficulties in supplying adequate greenhouse facilities to carry on research; inadequate light and temperature controls as well as a shortage of space preclude important experimentation on photosynthesis and growth as a function of biological and environmental stress.

At Stanford, geologists working on research which might provide new information on energy resources report that

> the quality of data taken in the department is not state of the art. Our equipment is held together with spit and string. We get around inadequately by borrowing or buying time on other equipment off campus from forty to two thousand miles away. . . . Laboratory analysis of field samples is seriously limited by lack of state-of-the-art electron beam, microanalysis facilities. Far greater efficiency and speed of program development would have been possible had more funds for equipment purchase and physical plant alterations been available.

Physicists at Northwestern remind us that

> without federal investment to assure the physical resources necessary for such areas, scientists' interest in them will be diverted, and U.S. competence in them will decline. Rebuilding such interests and competence will be very difficult and costly. The staggering cost of a lost generation of science in the People's Republic of China is a stark example of how difficult it is to rebuild interest and competence in science.

THE LEVEL OF NEED

The overall level of funding needs for equipment and facilities is not known, but a number of recent studies give some idea of the magnitude of the problem. The National Science Foundation and the National Academy of Sciences undertook a systematic effort to document equipment needs in academic laboratories in 1971–1972. They found an accumulated deficit of $276 million for the ten disciplines surveyed, with three-quarters of that deficit representing new equipment needs and one-quarter covering the replacement of worn-out or obsolescent items.[9] In 1977, *Research Universities and the National Interest* estimated that $100 million would be needed for three years to reduce a backlog in equipment needs at the major research universities and that $150 million a year should be provided for the renovation of university research facilities.[10]

In 1980, Congress directed the National Science Foundation to develop measures of "the status of scientific instrumentation in the United States and of the current and projected need for scientific and technological instrumentation." NSF has contracted for a feasibility study to determine how such data might be developed for the academic sector.

During fiscal year 1978, approximately $280 million was expended at Ph.D.-granting institutions in the United States for the purchase of scientific research equipment. Sixty-five percent of equipment purchases made from current funds was financed by the federal government (59 percent at public institutions, 75 percent at private institutions). Half was for the life sciences, 19 percent for engineering, and 16 percent for the physical sciences. Nine percent was for items costing $50,000 or more, although for electrical and computer engineering and chemistry that proportion was 27 percent. Expenditures for separately budgeted scientific research equipment from current funds constituted about 6 percent of all R&D expenditures at these institutions.[11]

---

[9]National Academy of Sciences, *Survey of Research Equipment Needs in Ten Academic Disciplines* (Washington, D.C., 1972).

[10]*Research Universities and the National Interest: A Report by Fifteen University Presidents* (New York: The Ford Foundation, 1977), pp. 56–57.

[11]Irene L. Gomberg and Frank Atelsek, *Expenditures for Scientific Research Equip-*

A 1979 survey by Princeton University of nine universities responsible for some 15 percent of federally sponsored academic research and development showed that they had spent over $225 million on research equipment and facilities in the past five years, but they had identified another $225 million in unmet needs—necessary projects for which they had as yet been unable to secure funding. These same universities estimated a need of $515 million (in 1979 dollars) over the next three to five years to bring their facilities and instrumentation up to modern standards.

To provide adequate research facilities, the fifteen universities surveyed by the AAU in 1981 estimated that they would need almost $765 million (in 1981 dollars) over the next three years merely to allow their faculty now in place to carry out their research effectively. This is nearly double their combined expenditures during the previous four years. These are needs which have been documented by officials at these fifteen universities rather than researchers' "wish lists." If the figures are extrapolated for the top 100 research universities and colleges (ranked by FY 1979 R&D funds received), it seems likely that the total funding needed would exceed $4 billion. Even allowing for some degree of overstatement, these estimates demonstrate the magnitude of the problem.

Almost 30 percent of the total projected needs for facility modernization is related to new government safety and health regulations. The American Council on Education estimated several years ago that simply coming into compliance with occupational safety and health standards would cost the nation's colleges and universities $3.6 billion. In a study requested by Congress, the National Center for Education Statistics estimated that the costs of compliance with Section 504 of the Rehabilitation Act of 1973 will exceed $560 million.

---

ment at Ph.D.-Granting Institutions, FY 1978, Higher Education Panel Report Number 47 (Washington, D.C.: American Council on Education, March 1980).

MEETING THE NEEDS

No matter how the needs are calculated, it is clear that the universities will not be able to undertake the new building and renovation needed to upgrade and modernize their facilities, nor to purchase the state-of-the-art instrumentation needed by their researchers and graduate students, out of their own operating funds. Nor will federal research grants and contracts provide adequate funding for necessary equipment purchases under current programs.[12]

To enable the research universities to make the contributions to national security and productivity of which they are capable, a comprehensive national strategy for investment in the needed facilities and instrumentation must be developed. The solution to the problems described above will require sustained initiatives by the private sector and by state governments as well as by the federal government. A national investment strategy should take into account contributions by all sectors. The following recommendations are offered as starting points for the development of such a strategy.

Assessing the Need

Although the studies cited above give some indication of the seriousness of the present deficiencies in university research facilities and instrumentation, they are based on limited samples at particular points in time. A more thorough assessment of the total situation is needed, as well as periodic evaluation of the adequacy of research facilities

---

[12] As noted above, the percentage of NSF project support going to permanent equipment has been as low as 5.4 percent, although it is now at 13 percent. At NIH, percentages for equipment are only 5.5 percent. A 1971 report from the National Academy of Sciences noted that in national laboratories in Germany and Great Britain, 14 to 22 percent of total laboratory funding is earmarked for instrumentation, explaining in part the abundant anecdotal evidence of superior instrumentation resources abroad and the growing evidence that foreign laboratories are surpassing the capacity of American ones to do state-of-the-art research.

and equipment in future years. The leading executive agencies (the Office of Science and Technology Policy, the National Science Foundation, the Departments of Defense, Health and Human Services, and Agriculture, and the National Aeronautics and Space Administration) should undertake a complete assessment of current needs and should provide for an ongoing process for periodic evaluation in the future. As part of that process, they should solicit the views of industrial representatives, universities, and researchers.

Competitive Grant Programs

The government should establish competitive grant programs to meet facilities and major equipment needs. Two types of programs would be particularly helpful to complement existing federal research funding efforts.

☐ *National Science Foundation Facilities and Equipment Initiatives.* A special $100 million initiative was proposed for fiscal year 1982 for NSF to begin the rehabilitation of academic research laboratories ($75 million) and to upgrade the instructional equipment of engineering schools ($25 million). That proposal was later deferred under budgetary pressures. It should be restored as a priority initiative in fiscal year 1983.

☐ *Mission Agencies.* The mission agencies (the Departments of Defense, Energy, Health and Human Services, and Agriculture, and the National Aeronautics and Space Administration) depend on universities to carry out research and education directly related to agency missions and goals. They should develop research facilities and instrumentation renewal programs designed to meet the needs of those programs.

For instance, the Department of Defense (DOD) plays a leading role in the support of basic research in universities in key fields such as engineering, mathematics, and computer sciences. In 1979, for example, the department provided 36 percent of total federal R&D obligations to universities for engineering and 45 percent of total federal support for mathematics and computer sciences.[13] In fields such as these, DOD should address the priority facilities rehabilitation and equipment needs of university research laboratories that carry out DOD research programs.

To start, the department should undertake a new Facilities and Instrumentation Renewal Program funded at a significant annual level, perhaps equal to 25 percent of total DOD basic research support. A program funded at that level would permit an initial investment of about $180 million in FY 1982 to meet acute defense-related needs, which may total over $1 billion among the top 100 research universities for engineering laboratories alone. In view of such large estimates, a comprehensive strategy involving many agencies of government, industry, and others is both appropriate and necessary. A substantial commitment by the Department of Defense would provide needed leadership for such an effort.

Other mission agencies should undertake similar commitments. If the National Science Foundation and the major mission agencies play complementary roles, the federal government will then have in place a comprehensive and balanced set of facilities and instrumentation initiatives. Together they would go far toward addressing the diverse needs of the sciences and engineering while also ensuring that those fields of particular importance to the mission of each agency receive the special attention they require.

Sources of Flexible Funding Program

☐ *Biomedical Research Support Grants.* The importance of the NIH Biomedical Research Support Grant (BRSG) Program as a source of flexible funds for equipment for new investigators and new lines of research has been noted at the beginning of this chapter. As recommended by the NIH Division of Research Resources, funding for the BRSG Program should be increased to bring it up to at least

---

[13] National Science Foundation, *Federal Funds for Research and Development, Fiscal Years 1979, 1980, 1981.* Vol. 29, pp. 120–121.

4 percent of NIH research grants. In addition, a shared instrument grant program should be established within the BRSG Program.

☐ *The National Science Foundation.* The National Science Foundation should establish a program similar to the BRSG Program but targeted to instrumentation needs. Funds would be awarded to institutions in proportion to total NSF support received in order to strengthen the research capacities of institutions doing research under NSF grants.

Such funds should be used by the institution to support the purchase and operation of equipment not provided for under individual grants, for example, the costs of providing laboratory equipment and technical and research assistants for new investigators or equipment which will be shared by several investigators or several departments. They could provide instrumentation for senior investigators seeking to branch into new areas, meet matching requirements for the special instrumentation funding programs and other grants, fund the facilities renovation and site preparation often required with the acquisition of new instrumentation, purchase support equipment, and meet operation and maintenance costs.

Under such a program, the instrumentation funds would follow the peer-reviewed, sponsored research funds awarded by NSF. The program would operate on each campus under the guidance of a university committee of faculty and research administrators who are in the best position to evaluate the instrumentation needs unique to their institution.

Such a source of supplemental, flexible funding would allow researchers and their institutions to respond quickly to unanticipated needs, to capitalize on unique local strengths and opportunities, and yet to remain fully accountable for federal research funds. This mechanism would have an immediate and direct salutary effect on the chronic instrumentation problems unsolved by existing programs. Funding should be at a level of $50 million annually.

*Additional Support for Instrumentation Through the
Project System*

☐ The size of individual awards from NSF and other
Federal agencies should be increased and a larger percentage
of funds should be allocated to the development, acquisition, and maintenance of instrumentation. The chemistry
division of NSF has in recent years doubled the percentage
of project grant funds allocated to instrumentation; other
programs should pursue similar policies. Agencies should
also provide greater support for operation and maintenance costs and should encourage effective sharing of instrumentation across project lines.

Special Instrumentation Funding Programs

☐ The special instrumentation funding programs should
be strengthened and made more flexible. The matching requirements should be changed to enable each institution to
contribute to the effective utilization of the instrumentation
in ways most appropriate to the particular circumstances
under which it operates. In particular, university contributions toward instrument operation and maintenance should
be calculated as part of the matching commitment. Such a
policy would help to assure that major instrumentation
would be available for effective use throughout its expected
lifetime.

Incentives to Industries and to the States

☐ Industries should be provided with tax incentives to
encourage their joining with universities and the federal
government to renew the nation's university research laboratories. As noted in Chapter 3, industry benefits directly
from the research and training provided by universities. In
recognition of that fact, industry has been an important
contributor of research equipment to many university laboratories. A few industries donate funds to help maintain
the equipment, but that is rarer than researchers would
like. One industry last year donated several million dollars in equipment to a university "based on the premise

that industry should support university sciences because universities are the principal source of training for people industry will eventually hire."[14] Many industries donate equipment or funds for equipment in the $30,000–150,000 range, sometimes, but not primarily, for research of interest to that industry. Harvard University has recently announced a grant of $50 million from a German chemical firm to Massachusetts General Hospital to underwrite a new laboratory of molecular biology in return for the opportunity to take first rights to market inventions developed during research.

Variation in the experience of universities with attracting industrial donations is great. An informal survey of such relationships carried out by the AAU in 1979 in conjunction with its survey of instrumentation needs indicated that a great deal depends on the relationships established between individual scientists and departments and individual researchers in industry. Faculty consultantships with industry are perhaps the most common contacts. Some university departments have established advisory committees that include industry and business representatives who consult on their needs. Within three years of the establishment of such a committee by the chemistry department at one major West Coast university, industrial contributions increased tenfold, from an annual average of from $30,000–40,000 to $350,000 a year, mostly in unrestricted funds used to acquire equipment.

☐ Since industry and, therefore, national productivity benefit directly from the research and training provided by research universities, Congress should provide incentives to industry for donating state-of-the art research and instructional equipment.

☐ States also might be encouraged, perhaps through matching programs, to assist in the renewal of research and teaching laboratories at institutions that contribute highly educated scientists and engineers to the state.

---

[14] Association of American Universities, *The Scientific Instrumentation Needs of Research Universities*, background papers.

In short, both industries and the states should be provided with incentives to attract their participation as active partners with the federal government and the universities in the proposed investment plan. Only such a partnership can ensure that the nation's university research laboratories are enabled to make the fullest possible contribution to the national research effort.

SHARING INSTRUMENTATION AND FACILITIES

One answer to the problem of providing access to the increasingly expensive facilities and instrumentation needed for state-of-the-art research is the sharing of such resources among researchers working on different grants, among departments, and among institutions. Such sharing is often established on an informal basis among colleagues; in recent years it has been encouraged by several federal programs and policies. The Biomedical Research Support Grants of the National Institutes of Health and the former National Science Foundation's Institutional Improvement for Science Program have provided flexible funds that have been used for centrally shared core facilities and instrument support shops, among other purposes. Block-funded research centers facilitate the acquisition, maintenance, and sharing of instrumentation, as do federally supported and operated research centers. Both kinds of facilities, however, are restricted to a few disciplines and a few universities. Sharing within and among departments may be made easier by new grant procedures that permit centralized administration of and accounting for a number of related grants.

In 1978 the National Science Foundation established a Regional Instrumentation Program to provide regional access to state-of-the-art instrumentation in mass spectrometry, nuclear magnetic resonance, lasers, isotope-dating and trace-element analysis, high-resolution electron microscopy, and surface analysis. Fourteen centers have been established with funding of about $20 million from 1978 to 1982; over the same four years operating expenses have been about $1.4 million for each center. Usually researchers must travel to the centers to use the facilities, although in one case (the San Francisco Laser Center) equipment can be loaned to laboratories for periods of up to one year.

As the AAU study on instrumentation pointed out, "at some level of cost, it is clear that regional or national facilities are necessary, that the instrumentation required to support research is simply too expensive to continue to exist under the purview of the individual researcher, a single department, or even a single institution."[15] Nevertheless, there are costs associated with sharing facilities and instrumentation. Even for interdepartmental sharing within the same university, investigators may be uninformed about instrumentation newly acquired by other departments and may object to the need to leave their own laboratories to work in another building. When facilities are located off campus, investigators complain about the inconvenience and cost of traveling to other institutions or to regional instrumentation centers. They believe that the distances involved make it difficult for graduate students to receive training at regional centers. Many express concern because instruments committed to a broad range of user needs often cannot be modified to meet highly specialized research requirements. Some believe that that fact and the considerable investment of time and money required to work through regional or national facilities make researchers reluctant to undertake high-risk experiments and lead them to settle for safer, less innovative research. Investigators also complain about limited access to shared instrumentation. Those limits and the delays in obtaining analyses of samples sent to off-campus facilities may cause delays in research.

☐ The central policy issue in the question of shared facilities and instrumentation is how best to deliver technology at the cutting edge of science to those researchers who can make the fullest possible contribution to scientific

---

[15] Ibid., p. 8.

knowledge. Careful assessment is needed of the levels of cost at which sharing is necessary and the problems involved are justified. Equally careful consideration must be given to the most effective location of shared facilities, to their capacity in terms of numbers of researchers whose needs can be accommodated, and to the processes by which projects are approved. The National Science Foundation should work with the mission agencies, the Office of Science and Technology Policy, the National Association of Science, disciplinary associations, and individual institutions and researchers to examine these questions and to ensure the most effective distribution of funds for research facilities and instrumentation.

CHAPTER SIX

INTERNATIONAL AND FOREIGN AREA
STUDIES AND RESEARCH

For a set of institutions reputed to be highly resistant to change, the nation's research universities look considerably different today from the way they did three decades ago. The most notable difference, of course, is their remarkable growth in the fields of science and technology. In some instances, this development followed, and even was driven by, the logic of scientific progress, most notably in fundamental physics and biology. In others, the driving force was a national purpose that was only coincidentally related either to institutional purposes or to the intellectual requirements of science. The most notable case was the large injection of federal support into training and research programs in the physical sciences and engineering as a consequence of national goals in military security and space exploration.

The developments in science and technology are visible and frequently dramatic and colorful, and so they have claimed much public attention. But another profoundly important change that has taken place in the research universities during this period has been their dramatically increased capacity to teach and engage in inquiry about societies other than their own and cultures other than those of the United States and Western Europe.

The size and quality of the enterprise that has been created are impressive. Its creation is an achievement that belies the image of the university as an institution so encrusted with tradition as to be impervious to change. A recent review of international studies programs points out: "In 1940, there were probably not more than 225 faculty members in the entire country prepared—not suggesting competent—to teach what we now call International Studies; today at any one of twenty universities there are that many faculty prepared to do so."[1]

There are now about 9,000 persons teaching international and foreign area studies in institutions of higher education. About a third of those are clustered in the major research universities, where fully one-third of the faculty in the humanities and social sciences teaches courses in international subjects, not counting the traditional offerings in Western European history and culture.

In short, a shift of focus of very dramatic proportions has occurred in the *teaching* composition of faculties and, consequently, in the teaching and research agendas of the research universities. Why this has happened, where the effort now stands, and what its future might be are all questions of considerable importance for the universities and for the nation.

So much effort has been spent in recent years in bruising battles to sustain the level of federal appropriations for international studies that it is easy to overlook the fact that the growth of international studies predates the involvement of the federal government. The first significant support of international studies came from organized philanthropy. These early contributions were critical because they gave impetus to the leading universities. The programs that they helped to build later served as examples and as points of departure for their successors.

Those successors began to emerge in the 1950s when the

---

[1] Elinor G. Barber and Warren Ilchman, "The Preservation of the Cosmopolitan Research University in the United States," *Annals of the American Academy of Political and Social Science,* May 1980, p. 3.

Ford Foundation decided to make the development of university-based programs of international and foreign area studies a major priority. From 1951 to 1975 the Ford Foundation spent $340 million in that effort. It is one of the more extraordinary episodes in the history of American philanthropy. In size, in the length of time over which it was sustained, and in its effect on the institutions which were its targets, the Ford Foundation effort has had no equals. Compared with it, even the programs of the federal government seem modest. From 1958 to 1978, the government through its chief vehicle in support of international studies, the National Defense Education Act (NDEA), spent $229 million in pursuit of its goals.

The principal stimulus for both efforts was the realization that the world outside of America's borders had become both more important and more threatening and that as a nation we were ill prepared to deal with it. We lacked adequate training in most of the world's languages, had few specialists in world areas of critical importance to the nation, and had only a limited capacity to train more. The common premise of the two efforts was that it was necessary to build the institutional capacity to repair those deficiencies. Much of the development, therefore, was aimed at building strength in the study of world areas that had hitherto suffered from at least relative neglect, specifically, the USSR and Eastern Europe, Africa, the Middle East, East Asia, Latin America, and South and Southeast Asia.

It is important to be clear about the motives for this extraordinary growth. The Ford Foundation to some extent and the government even more so were strongly moved by the need to develop specific kinds of research and training capacity in order to promote the improvement of American foreign policy and hence the enhancement of American security.

On the other side of the relationship, university faculty and administrators were certainly not unmindful of the instrumental value of improving international studies. Indeed, many made that point at every opportunity. But many also saw the need and the chance to build aspects of institutional strength whose past absence had limited the intellectual power and range of the academy.

There is no need to overdraw the difference in the two perspectives. It is important only as it helps to explain the events of the last decade. In the early 1970s the Ford Foundation decided to bring to a close its program of institutional grants for international studies programs. That decision rested on the reasonable expectation that government funding for those programs under NDEA, the International Education Act, or both would provide the means of sustenance for the programs that had been built in the previous decades. That expectation was unrealized. From 1969–1978, in fact, government funding fell drastically in real dollars, depreciating by fully 58 percent from $20.5 million to $8.5 million ($15 million in 1980 dollars).

Many reasons account for the decline. It began in 1971 as part of a broad move by the Nixon administration toward revenue sharing and away from categorical programs—a move given added impetus in the case of higher education by administration anger at the antiwar movement. The recession of 1973–1975 had a further dampening effect on attitudes toward such expenditures. In addition, international education funding was without important bureaucratic allies: its sponsor was a politically weak Office of Education, its chief adversary was a powerful Office of Management and Budget, and its main potential beneficiary, the Department of State, was uninvolved and uninterested. As a result of all of these factors, there were annual appropriations battles over relatively small amounts of money. Perhaps part of the explanation for the decline in federal support for these programs was that the payoff from the enterprise was oversold, that the immediate value for foreign policy turned out to be less than advertised, and that no satisfactory justification was put forward once that became evident. In a real sense, funding for international studies shared the fate of the optimistic internationalism of the postwar period: when the world turned out to be less tractable than it was thought to be, those programs that were the product of the earlier assumptions paid the price.

Adequate, indeed compelling, justifications for international studies programs do exist, and it is essential that they be advanced as the basis for sound and reliable policies that will sustain what has been created. The value of strong programs of international and foreign area studies can be viewed from four perspectives: their value to the universities of which they are a part, their value to the government, their value to the private sector, and their value to society at large.

THE UNIVERSITY OUTLOOK

The need for strong programs of international and foreign area studies as integral parts of the research universities rests essentially on the same justification as the study of physics or chemistry, philosophy or economics. The root purpose of fundamental research is to increase understanding of the phenomena being studied, based on abiding faith supported by considerable evidence that enhanced understanding of the world will lead eventually to important practical benefits. University faculties and curricula have long reflected the belief that the study of the man-made universe is as central to the university's purposes as are discoveries of the physical and biological universe. What is of more recent vintage is an appreciation that the achievement of that purpose requires the ability to study man and his works wherever he and they exist.

That is why the leaders of the nation's most important universities have devoted so much of their limited time and influence to efforts to increase international studies appropriations to totals that, in comparison with science funding, seem miniscule. The struggle was deemed worthwhile in order to prevent a return to the narrower and more cramped outlook of the past. The development of a broader vision has important implications for public policy as well.

THE GOVERNMENT OUTLOOK

Of all the institutions of our society, the federal government has perhaps the largest direct stake in the health of research and training programs in international and foreign area studies. Research done for the President's Commission on Foreign Language and International Studies by the Rand Corporation[2] showed that there are 30,000–40,000 positions in the federal government that call for foreign language competence and that 14,000 to 19,000 of those also demand analytic skills with respect to foreign countries. The federal government is, thus, a major employer of people with these skills.

How well is the demand being met? The answer appears to be tolerably well in the main Western European languages, although there is room for improvement, but much less well in some of the more important but difficult languages, such as Chinese, Japanese, and Arabic. In fact, the government is able to fill less than 40 percent of the available positions requiring those languages with people who meet the level of minimum professional proficiency in speaking and reading. The problem is compounded for positions that require substantive knowledge of the economics, politics, or cultures of other countries in addition to language proficiency.[3]

The problem is in part one of insufficient supply, but it is exacerbated by personnel policies that are at odds with the need. Specialists are not highly valued in the career service. Advancement goes to those who develop managerial skills. This has the perverse effect of forcing the best of the specialists to choose between leaving government in order to practice their specialty or leaving their specialty in order to advance in government. Since the government is

---

[2] Sue E. Berryman et al., *Foreign Language and International Studies Specialists: The Marketplace and National Policy* (Santa Monica: Rand Corporation, 1979).

[3] Robert A. Ward, "International Studies and the National Interest: Too Little but Not Too Late," *Washington Quarterly*, Summer 1980, pp. 164–173.

such a voracious user of internationally trained talent, it has a clear interest in assuring the adequacy of the supply and in arranging its personnel policies intelligently. The problems in this area, while difficult, are solvable by known means, assuming the desire to solve them exists.

The federal government as consumer of research, however, faces more formidable difficulties. It is necessary to say candidly and publicly what has long been said privately: the government has been short-sighted and unintelligent in its approach to scholarly research. It has been an impatient and inattentive user. Policy-level officers in agencies with international problems tend to be overwhelmed by immediate demands and have little patience for academic research. When academic specialists are brought into the policymaking process, either full time or as consultants, they have no more of a claim to "right" answers than does anyone else, since "right" in the short run frequently depends on sound political judgment as much as on expert knowledge.

The problem is an old one, which in its most general form concerns the value of the social sciences for policymaking in all aspects of government, not just foreign policy. It is more acute in the area of foreign policy because those responsible for its conduct have, on the whole, been far less thoughtful about the uses of social science than have their domestic counterparts. Foreign affairs officers depend heavily on reports from the field and the rapid evaluation of such information. Their decisions tend to be less informed by long-term data-gathering and by trend and retrospective analysis than are, for example, policies with respect to the economy or welfare programs, agriculture, banking, health, transportation, or any of a host of other domestic issues. Both a symbol and a cause of the problem can be seen in the fact that in 1967 all federal expenditures for grant and contract research on foreign affairs amounted to only $40 million. By 1976, the total (in 1967 dollars) was less than $20 million. Furthermore, the Department of State, the lead foreign policy agency, has no grant-making authority. Thus, even if it were disposed to deal with universities as other agencies do, it lacks the authority to use the most flexible instrument for doing so.

What is lost by such attitudes and the policies they produce is the possibility of improving, if only peripherally, the conduct of foreign policy. But to characterize the loss as marginal is not to say that it is trivial. The fundamentals of political conflict will always remain political and therefore beyond the reach of research, no matter how refined and sophisticated. But political strategy that is informed by a sophisticated knowledge of the institutions, practices, and characteristic habits of thought of allies and adversaries is more likely to be grounded in what is possible and less likely to stumble over its own mistaken assumptions.

In order to move in that direction, government officials need to take a long-range and more expansive view of the nature and benefits of scholarship. Stimulating research on Islamic nationalism may not provide answers to dilemmas of foreign policy in the Middle East any more than research in high energy physics can be expected to solve the energy crisis. However, both are entitled to a similar act of faith, namely, that knowledge is to be preferred to ignorance because it may reveal possibilities that ignorance keeps hidden. Policies based on that premise would, over time, produce mutual respect between the federal government and universities in the critical area of foreign affairs and would redound to the benefit of both.

The role of government in insuring the productivity of university programs of international and foreign area studies is limited but extremely important. The basic responsibility for maintaining the core belongs to the universities, but the government is responsible for enabling the most productive use of the resulting resources. Since the first flush of post-Sputnik enthusiasm, the federal government has acknowledged that responsibility only grudgingly. The areas of that responsibility are outlined below.

Language and Area Centers

The Language and Area Centers have become the chief instruments for organizing efforts on campus that use the talents of faculty who are otherwise located in a variety of separate disciplines. Support of the centers makes possible interaction among disparate points of approach and makes possible, too, a broader reach than scholars in individual disciplines can achieve alone.

Increasingly the resources of universities are strained to meet the fundamental responsibilities of financing faculty, facilities, and basic library costs. The additional costs attendant to maintaining the center structures are necessarily of a lower priority at budget time. Government funding, thus, is critical if the structure so slowly and painfully erected over the years is not to crumble. It is especially reassuring, therefore, that the Reagan administration and Congress agreed to protect the appropriation for Title VI of the Higher Education Act from which these centers are financed. If that act represents renewed regard for the importance of international studies among Washington policymakers, it will indeed be welcome news. Language and area centers contain the nation's primary concentration of talent for research and graduate instruction; they are the spring that feeds all other parts of the system.

It is important that the currently fashionable dispute between the virtues of the "area" as opposed to the "problem-oriented" or "functional" approaches not interfere with this important initiative. That dispute is no more likely to produce intellectually satisfactory results than did the earlier battles between the area approach and the academic disciplines. It is sufficient that sound policy, academic and governmental, recognize that the accumulation of knowledge and the solution of problems are not unrelated activities, that the former without the latter is mere pedantry while the latter without the former is little better than guesswork. The task of policy is to bring the two into fruitful interaction.

The language and area centers now in existence and

those that may be created should be viewed as national in their scope and reach. Where cooperation between institutions is possible, including the establishment of joint centers, it should be encouraged as a way of taking advantage of complementary resources. If the centers are seen as truly national facilities, there is only one standard of judgment for determining where they are to be located: that is a dispassionate assessment of the present quality and future prospects of the resources available for the center. Any lesser standard will necessarily dilute the contributions that these important organizations can make.

Libraries

The major library collections in the international fields, particularly those involving non-Western language collections, are resources of incalculable value. They were built over long periods of time primarily by private and state government funds, and responsibility for their maintenance continues to reside primarily in those places. However, circumstances have changed dramatically in the last decade. Inflation abroad, combined with the unfavorable exchange rate for the dollar in most international markets, have driven up the cost of buying materials abroad, and inflation at home has raised the cost of processing materials for use. Valuable collections can too easily fall into disrepair unless needed materials are acquired on a timely basis. The problem requires two complementary approaches.

Chapter 4 deals in more detail with the general problem of interlibrary cooperation. The need for cooperative efforts is multiplied in the international area where costs are greater and materials may be scarce. The establishment of a National Periodicals Center with responsibility for collecting foreign periodicals would spare many libraries the need to acquire and maintain expensive serial runs from abroad.

As another approach to lowering the cost of collecting, regional library sharing programs should be explicitly encouraged by a program of government grants for acquisitions, processing, and sharing of materials. In appropriate cases, and at least for the purpose of testing the value of the incentive, these grants might be made a part of the Language and Area Center grants for those institutions that are prepared to undertake or to expand cooperative programs.

Graduate Financial Aid

Financial support for graduate students in international and foreign area programs should be incorporated into a broader national program of graduate financial aid of the kind described in Chapter 2. One special requirement of such study argues for limited special treatment, namely, the need for most students of area and international subjects to do dissertation research, advanced language study, or both abroad. Center grants should include funds to aid students with the added costs imposed by that requirement.

International Research

The policy of the government with respect to the support of research in international and foreign affairs is a shambles. Indeed, it hardly exists. The subject is far too important to be allowed to continue in its present condition.

It is instructive to recall that in 1975, Secretary of State Henry Kissinger appointed a government-academic task force on mid-term research for foreign policy. Its charge consisted of (1) continuing and extending the dialogue between scholars and foreign policymakers, and (2) designing and implementing research on mid-term problems of foreign policy. It was a promising initiative, but in the end it served its first purpose far better than its second, partly because the attempt to define the need for research, and therefore its value, as lying along a time line that runs from short term to long term points consideration of the issue in the wrong direction. The focus must be on the need for knowledge of political, economic, and social processes embedded in the cultural contexts in which they exist in the real world. It is from those processes that policy problems emerge, and it is within them that workable responses must be found.

There are corresponding problems on the university

side. In the international fields, perhaps above all others, academic energies have been devoted to essentially unproductive battles over research methods and over the best ways to organize research and teaching. As a consequence, the more profound question—how does research, however organized and conducted, justify a claim on public resources?—goes largely unaddressed. The effort to identify and articulate the social and policy value of international research is important. It has hardly even begun.

The research that leads to the knowledge of political, economic, and social processes on which policy must be based is the kind of research that university faculty do best and that, moreover, is not done elsewhere. It is research that finds its own uses. Elaboration and specification of those truths is the responsibility of scholars. It is a task that might well be undertaken jointly by the Association of American Universities and the Social Science Research Council.

The main task within the government is to encourage the Department of State to take seriously a complementary responsibility. Federal research policy on international matters has suffered from the lack of a "lead agency," an agency whose need for research defines an area of support and around which other supporting agencies like the National Science Foundation and the Department of Education can fit complementary programs. The Department of State is the logical agency to fill that role. Therefore, the State Department, in consultation with other agencies having important international responsibilities and with the assistance of academic specialists, is the proper agency to put in motion a process which can continuously define and redefine the intellectual base which supports the conduct of foreign affairs. The purpose of those deliberations would be to define research topics related to current policy issues. The results of that deliberative process should serve to inform a program of grants and contracts designed to improve the base of knowledge in the relevant fields. Here as elsewhere, knowledge finds its own uses, often quite unpredictable ones. The haphazard, indeed indifferent, approach to the generation of knowledge on the part of the agency responsible for the conduct of foreign policy has been and continues to be dangerously short-sighted.

Although the State Department must take the lead in defining and executing government research policy, all agencies with significant international responsibilities must be involved. Therefore, it is imperative that the government and the universities come to terms over the role of the CIA in respect to universities. At present, a number of issues that are in principle separable are so intertwined that none can be addressed effectively. There are important matters at stake in the resolution of such issues as the propriety of CIA debriefing of faculty who travel abroad and of secret CIA recruiting on campus. Some faculty whose research takes them abroad have argued that any scholarly involvement with the CIA—or other intelligence agencies, for that matter—compromises the access to foreign sources of those who are entirely innocent of such involvement. It is clear that it will not be easy to reach satisfactory agreement on these matters. No matter how difficult and contentious those issues are, however, it remains true that the CIA, in its capacity as gatherer and evaluator of intelligence, is one of the largest and most sophisticated governmental users of scholarly research about international matters.

The nation's capacity for gleaning and interpreting intelligence rests on a base of knowledge that is generated and disseminated freely by the usual methods of scholarly communication. It is not hard to think of organizational forms that would enhance the process. One already exists and may well serve as a model for other programs. During the Ford administration, the Department of Defense, acting in cooperation with eleven universities and the American Association for the Advancement of Slavic Studies, agreed to support a program of basic research in the Soviet Union. The program was funded at the level of one million dollars per year. A new corporation, the National Council for Soviet and East European Research, with trustees drawn from university faculties, was created to administer the program. The Department of State and the Arms Control and Disarmament Agency later joined as supporters of the program. In 1981, the Secretary of Defense, acting in response to budgetary pressures, announced that the DOD would no longer support the program. Harvard University President Derek Bok, writing on behalf of the original eleven universities, a group that had grown to thirty-one by then, urged the Secretary of Defense to reconsider:

> This undertaking is unique. For the first time in the nation's history, major research universities, the professional association of Slavic scholars, and the Department of Defense have joined together to create a long-range national program of fundamental research on the USSR, defined and conducted in close consultation with each other, and systematically oriented toward issues bearing on the national security of the United States.[4]

In response to President Bok's appeal, the Deputy Secretary of Defense wrote:

> We have carefully reviewed this matter and recognize the importance of the work that has been done under the council's auspices. . . . I am proposing that the DOD allocate the council $500,000 for FY 1981 provided that an additional $500,000 can be located from other sources in the U.S. government. The director of Central Intelligence has indicated a willingness to try to provide the additional funds.[5]

The National Council for Soviet and East European Research agreed to the proposed funding on the understanding that the selection of projects and the monitoring of research be in the hands of academics, that the research supported be open and unclassified, and that the council would report to an interagency committee and not just to the two financial sponsors.

There is no reason why such an arrangement cannot work to everyone's benefit. It is an arrangement worth

---

[4]Letter from Derek Bok et al. to Caspar Weinberger, April 7, 1981.
[5]Letter from Frank Carlucci to Derek Bok, May 15, 1981.

watching closely and emulating widely. An active and vigorous State Department would take the initiative in putting together similar arrangements in other areas of mutual interest.

Development Assistance

A special focus of research and training is that which is directly relevant to the American interest in assisting the process of economic and social development in the less developed countries. Such assistance through research and training in agriculture and nutrition has a long history, involving primarily land-grant universities. Those universities and others have participated effectively in efforts to build educational institutions as well. Research universities of all kinds have addressed development issues on both regional or global bases and on a country basis by research and training in health, population, communication and information, energy planning, environmental protection, and natural resources management.

A new focus of federal attention has been the importance of strengthening U.S. efforts in the field of transfer of science and technology to developing countries. Increased opportunities for collaborative research by U.S. and developing country institutions are needed, as are mechanisms to increase cooperation with the "middle income" countries which are no longer eligible for programs of the U.S. Agency for International Development. The role of the private sector, including both universities and business, can be crucial in helping other countries to develop their own scientific and technological capabilities. The government needs to develop organizational forms to assist the research universities in bringing to bear their resources in such assistance. Such efforts should emphasize coordination of the work of those in science and technology with the work of the country and area specialists who know the culture, politics, and economics of the regions involved and of those who study development as a process.

Because of the breadth of their own programs and personnel, research universities are in a unique position to aid in the development of educational institutions in other countries. The most efficient means of accomplishing this is by specific and targeted agreements between counterpart institutions in the United States and developing countries. These agreements include cooperative programs of faculty and student exchange, research, curriculum and program planning, resource development, manpower planning and development, and management and administration. The federal government will benefit from providing the relatively modest travel and other funds which are essential to support such agreements.

THE PRIVATE SECTOR OUTLOOK

The Rand Corporation study conducted for the President's Commission on Foreign Language and International Studies concludes:

> Business and industry attach a low priority to language, cultural and area skills, largely because English is so widely used in international business that those skills are rarely essential. When they are, firms have little difficulty in hiring foreign nationals. Furthermore, U.S. firms are depending more and more upon foreign nationals in their foreign operations, thus reducing the need for Americans to have foreign language skills.[6]

This attitude flies in the face of good sense. As the President's Commission reported:

> International trade involves one out of every eight of America's manufacturing jobs and one out of three acres of America's farmland. American investment abroad is around $300 billion, and foreign investment in the United States is an estimated $245 billion. The thirteen largest American banks now derive almost 50 percent of their total earnings from overseas credits. Approximately 35,000 American companies have

---

[6]Berryman et al., *Foreign Language*, p. 123.

overseas operations, and 20,000 concerns export products or services to foreign markets.[7]

It is very hard to accept the conclusion that such extensive involvement in overseas markets, which originated at a time of unquestioned American economic and political dominance, can be sustained without intelligent strategies based on reliable knowledge of foreign markets and the political, legal, and social structures in which they are embedded. To assume that it can reflects the economic equivalent of the immediate postwar political myopia that led leaders to believe that American military power was sufficient to produce all desired political results.

It is in the interest of American business, and particularly that sizable fraction that is heavily engaged in international markets, to ensure that the institutional capacity for producing trained intelligence and basic knowledge remains vital. From that capacity flows the ability to respond to new manpower needs as they arise, the ability to generate and transmit the knowledge of foreign cultures and institutions and of international processes that, over time, makes business decisions more soundly based. American business may continue to use indigenous personnel in operating positions in their overseas operations, but foreign nationals cannot be relied on for systematic knowledge of their societies of the kind routinely available to businessmen—American and foreign—in America about America. The research capacity for generating such knowledge simply does not exist outside the United States and a few centers in Western Europe and Japan, and it is not likely to come into being in the foreseeable future. If that capacity is eroded in the leading American universities, there is no available substitute.

It is also in the interest of American business to encour-

---

[7] *Strength Through Wisdom: A Critique of U.S. Capability*, Report to the President from the President's Commission on Foreign Language and International Studies (Washington, D.C.: U.S. Government Printing Office, November 1979), p. 125.

age the development of greater international sophistication in the curricula of business and law schools, the main sources of upper management for the next generation. Management of foreign affiliates by nationals of those countries is likely to run into trouble over the long run if it is not complemented by internationally sophisticated management at home.

Finally, individual firms, or perhaps sectors, will benefit in the long run from developing area- or function-specific relations with individual or small groups of institutions. Many businesses have profited by such connections in various fields of science and technology. Companies that now have or wish to develop an in-house social science capacity will be in the best position to profit from such arrangements because the evidence suggests that successful collaboration requires mutual respect based on mutual interests and professional competence on both sides.

In sum, those American corporations with the heaviest stake in international operations should take an active responsibility for preserving the leading university centers for training and research in international and foreign area studies. They need to view the support of research on international matters as they and others view research on matters of science and technology. It is not simply an act of philanthropy, but it is in a company's interest to encourage scholars whose work shows promise of contributing to the knowledge base on which its interests will depend in the future.

To further those purposes, it would be useful to hold one or more carefully prepared meetings involving corporate leaders responsible for their companies' international operations and leading scholars in international and foreign area studies. This approach has been tried in the fields of chemistry and chemical engineering with promising results. The Council on Foreign Language and International Studies (created in 1980), with its close links to the business and academic communities, would be an appropriate leader for coordinating such an effort, as would the Business–Higher Education Forum of the American Council on Education.

The academic community needs to take greater initiative in explaining the potential value of the mainstream of modern social science research to the interests of the business community. And it needs to be open to curriculum changes that will meet the perceived needs of business. Part B of Title VI of the 1980 Higher Education Act makes tangible the government's interest in enhancing cooperation between business and higher education in the sphere of international education and research. This new authority enables the government to match funds provided by businesses and institutions of higher learning that enter into joint agreements that will be beneficial and profitable to both sectors. Its effectiveness will depend on the willingness of firms or trade associations to fund their share of such agreements. It is an experiment worth trying.

CHAPTER SEVEN

SUMMARY OF RECOMMENDATIONS

This report describes some of the major challenges facing the research universities and the principles that should guide the response of the universities, the federal government, and the private sector in meeting those challenges. The details of specific proposals will be overtaken by time and events, but the principles on which they rest are more durable. The format of the text emphasizes the latter. For those readers who wish a quick review and a summary of the recommendations for discussion or action, we offer it here, divided by the sectors we see as responsible for initiating action. The recommendations are, of course, more fully comprehensible in the context in which they appear in the individual chapters.

The recommendations for government action, while modest enough by past standards, may seem unrealistically large in the present political and economic climate. And so they may be. But the needs they address are real and important, and the case for meeting those needs should be made in anticipation of the time when their urgency will be generally recognized.

THE FEDERAL GOVERNMENT

Advanced Graduate Training

The most important long-term goal of government policy in regard to graduate education should be to assure that an adequate fraction of the most able college graduates is able to pursue graduate study. Two programs are important for that goal:

☐ There should be no diminution of effort in the National Science Foundation's competitive graduate fellowship awards.

☐ The new National Graduate Fellows Program authorized by the 1980 Higher Education Act should be funded at a level adequate to support the authorized 450 four-year awards annually.

Two special needs require special action—the need to attract more minority students into graduate school and the need to solve the short-term problem of the shortage of Ph.D. engineers. We recommend:

☐ The financial barriers to graduate study for minority students should be removed through strengthening the Graduate and Professional Opportunities Program. GPOP should be fully funded, and allotments to institutions should not be limited to narrowly prescribed fields but should be available for support of the best minority and female students in the institution's applicant pool.

☐ The Department of Education should work toward a program similar to the National Science Foundation's Minority Graduate Fellowship Program.

The solution to the shortage of graduate engineers should be approached with caution, given the likelihood that the shortage will be of relatively short duration and that the system will adjust itself to a significant extent without government intervention. Industrial support for graduate engineering students and subsidized programs of advanced training for engineers employed in industry may help to solve the problems more economically and with less later disruption than would crash government programs.

☐ If careful monitoring shows that federal support for training high technology Ph.D.'s is needed, the best way to provide it would be through expansion of the NSF Graduate Fellowship Program for that purpose.

A combination of faculty hiring patterns during the expansion of the 1970s, expected lower undergraduate enrollments in the 1980s and 1990s, low rates of growth in research funding, and a later mandatory retirement age will create a difficult situation for younger scholars during the next fifteen or twenty years. The number of new faculty openings in certain fields and departments will probably be sharply reduced until the late 1990s. This situation has unhappy consequences not only for younger scholars but also for the intellectual life of the universities and for their efforts to bring more women and minorities on to their faculties. The goal of policy in this situation must not be to insulate individuals or institutions from the effects of long-term social change but to mitigate the damaging disruption to institutions that can be produced by too rapid rates of change. Although several recent committees and commissions have recommended government programs to enable institutions to bring young people on to their faculties earlier than would otherwise be possible, we believe that this problem is better addressed by the universities themselves, with assistance from the private sector. We do urge, however:

☐ There should be no further increase in the minimum legal age for mandatory retirement.

It is imperative that the effects of the 1982 change to a minimum mandatory faculty retirement age of seventy be absorbed and evaluated before further changes are made.

Industry-University Collaboration in Science

The potential advantages of the growing interest in collaboration between industry and research universities, in terms of increased scientific innovation and economic productivity, have led to a wide variety of proposed legislation to facilitate those relationships. We believe that caution is needed here in order to avoid premature closure on the best ways to foster cooperation. However, two kinds of proposals deserve immediate action:

☐ Business should be provided with tax incentives for the support of basic research in universities and for the donation of scientific equipment and funds for facilities.

☐ The rules and regulations governing the assignment of patent rights for inventions made with the aid of government funding should be made supportive of the aim of encouraging innovation as a major source of economic growth.

Research Libraries

The great research libraries of the nation which support research and teaching in all fields are on the verge of a revolution in the ways they provide access to their readers to needed research materials. Inflation has made it impossible for them to maintain complete collections in all fields, but new technological developments have made possible a degree of sharing which may help them to provide the same or better services to their users. The federal government can help to ensure an orderly transition in several ways:

☐ The National Endowment for the Humanities should establish an Office of Scholarly Communication to monitor technological change and its effects on the system of scholarly communication, as recommended by the National Enquiry into Scholarly Communication.

☐ Title II C of the Higher Education Act should be fully funded and should emphasize support of Centers of Special Responsibility voluntarily established by research libraries.

☐ Title II D of the Higher Education Act, which provides for a National Periodical System, should be funded; a board should be appointed promptly and an implementation study initiated.

☐ A means should be devised for the provision of federal funding to assist in the transition to a new technology for research libraries.

Research Facilities and Instrumentation

The erosion of the physical research base—facilities and equipment—in American universities has been well documented. There is considerable evidence that American university laboratories are falling behind their counterparts abroad in their ability to do state-of-the-art research because they lack the facilities and equipment needed to keep scientists at the cutting edge of their disciplines.

A number of new governmental initiatives have been proposed as a way of strengthening the university research base which is crucial to industrial productivity, national security, and the national well-being. Some of the most important include:

☐ Government agencies should make a coordinated effort to assess the total current level of need for university research facilities and instrumentation and should establish procedures for periodic evaluation in future years.

☐ Competitive grant programs should be established in the National Science Foundation and the mission agencies (Defense, Energy, Aeronautics and Space, National Institutes of Health) that are targeted on programs to refurbish and upgrade laboratories in the fields of science and engineering of primary significance to the agencies.

☐ Funding for the NIH Biomedical Research Support Grant Program should be increased to bring it up to at least 4 percent of NIH research grants. In addition, a shared instrument grant program should be established within the BRSG Program, as recommended by the NIH Division of Research Resources.

☐ A program similar to the BRSG Program but targeted to instrumentation needs should be established in the National Science Foundation. Funds would be awarded to institutions in proportion to total NSF support received. This would provide a source of important flexible funds for equipment which cannot be provided under direct grants.

☐ Additional support for instrumentation should be provided through the project system, with both additional funds and a greater percentage of funds allocated to the development, acquisition, and maintenance of instrumentation.

☐ The special instrumentation funding programs should be expanded, and the matching requirements should be made more flexible.

☐ Incentives should be provided to industries and to the states to encourage them to join with universities and the federal government in renewing the nation's university research laboratories.

International and Foreign Area Studies and Research

The U.S. government has a large stake in the health of research and training programs in international and foreign area studies. It is a major employer of people with foreign language and foreign area competence; it should be a major user of scholarly research on the political, economic, and cultural systems of other nations. Although the universities are responsible for maintaining the core of programs in international and foreign area studies, the government bears an important part of the responsibility for enabling the most productive use of these resources.

The Language and Area Centers contain the nation's primary concentration of talent for research and graduate instruction; they are the spring that feeds all other parts of the system. Government funding is critical in maintaining the centers which make possible a broader reach than scholars in individual disciplines can achieve alone.

☐ The Language and Area Centers should be funded at no less than current levels. They should be viewed as national in their scope and reach. Cooperation between institutions, including the establishment of joint centers, should be encouraged, as should regional library sharing programs.

☐ Financial support for graduate students in international and foreign area programs should be incorporated into a broader national program of graduate financial aid. However, grants to language and area centers should include funds to aid students with the added costs of dissertation research and advanced language study abroad.

Government policy on support of research on international and foreign affairs needs careful reexamination, both by scholars and by the government. Both the Department of State and the Central Intelligence Agency must find better ways to support and use scholarly analysis.

☐ The Department of State, in consultation with other agencies having important international responsibilities and with the assistance of academic specialists, should put in motion a process which can continuously define and redefine the intellectual base which supports the conduct of foreign affairs.

☐ It is imperative that the government and the universities come to terms over the role of the CIA in respect to universities.

One model for cooperation might be The National Council for Soviet and East European Research, an independent organization of scholars, which has been funded in the past by the Department of Defense, the Department of State, and the Arms Control and Disarmament Agency and which in the future is to be funded by DOD and the Central Intelligence Agency.

Research universities have played an important role in U.S. development assistance efforts, especially in agriculture and nutrition. With the new government focus on science and technology transfer for development, new methods of using university expertise must be developed.

☐ The government needs to develop organizational forms to ensure that the research universities can effectively assist American efforts to help less developed countries to develop their own scientific and technological capabilities.

☐ The government should provide the relatively modest travel and other funds essential to support links between U.S. universities and counterpart institutions in the developing countries.

INDUSTRY

Advanced Graduate Training

Because industry depends on universities to provide the trained manpower it needs in all areas—science, social science, and the professions—industry should pay special attention to the problems faced by graduate and professional schools in meeting the needs of graduate students and in assisting younger scholars who face a decade or more of reduced opportunities for research support and teaching positions. Specifically:

☐ Industry should cooperate with universities and with private foundations to assist in developing and financing thoughtful approaches to the career cycle problems that face some institutions and fields.

☐ Industry should also cooperate with universities in giving systematic attention to the generation of career patterns in which scholars and scientists will move among universities, industry, government, and other nonprofit institutions.

Industry-University Collaboration in Science

Many thoughtful people are beginning to place their hopes for improvements in the competitive position of American business and in the health of university-based science in the growing collaboration between business and universities. Much thought is needed about how to make these links productive. In particular:

☐ Industry should cooperate with universities in finding acceptable ways to deal with such matters as patents and licenses and the handling of proprietary information and its implications for freedom of publication.

☐ The principle of recognition of indirect costs should be included in all industry-university research agreements.

☐ Industries whose member firms are active collaborators with universities should recognize and give effect to a shared responsibility to maintain the invisible institutional underpinnings of the universities on which they depend for training and basic research.

The newly established Council for Chemical Research and its Chemical Sciences and Engineering Fund might serve as a good model for other industries.

Research Libraries

Research libraries support research not only in the academic community but also in business and industry, both by direct services to users and by supporting university training and research which are useful to industry. Industry should therefore accept the responsibility to increase its support of these vital institutions. Specifically:

☐ Industry should increase the size of contributions to research libraries, and in particular to joint projects and to those which will have an impact beyond individual institutions.

☐ Industry should join foundations and state and federal governments in helping to fund the transition to a new technology for research libraries and should be active collaborators in the design and use of that new technology.

Research Facilities and Instrumentation

Many industrial firms are already major donors of research equipment and of funds for research facilities at universities. Such donations and funding should be increased wherever possible. That would be facilitated if the government provided tax incentives for such contributions. Therefore:

☐ Industry should cooperate with universities in working to obtain legislation providing tax incentives for industry contributions to universities of research instrumentation and for funds for maintenance of equipment and research facilities.

International and Foreign Area Studies and Research

The extensive involvement of American business and industry in overseas markets cannot be sustained without intelligent strategies based on reliable knowledge of foreign markets and of the political, legal, and social structure in which they are embedded. It is thus in the interest of American business to ensure that the institutional capacity for producing those with trained intelligence and basic knowledge remains vital. It is also in their interest to encourage the development of greater international sophistication in the curricula of business and law schools, the main sources of upper management for the next generation. Finally, individual firms or sectors would benefit from developing area- or function-specific relations with individual or small groups of institutions. Therefore, we recommend the following actions:

☐ American corporations with the heaviest stake in international operations should take an active responsibility for preserving the leading university centers for training and research in international and foreign area studies.

☐ Industry should cooperate with the National Council on Foreign Language and International Studies and the Business-Higher Education Forum of the American Council on Education to sponsor meetings in which corporate leaders responsible for their companies' international operations and leading scholars in international studies and research can explore areas of mutual interest.

☐ Industry should work with university faculties to develop curricular changes and other programs to enhance the international aspects of business education. Industry should provide funds to match those provided under Part B of Title VI of the 1980 Higher Education Act.

THE RESEARCH UNIVERSITIES

Clearly the primary responsibility for maintaining the health and vitality of the research universities lies with the institutions themselves, with the faculty, administration, and boards of trustees who must guide their development. In each of the areas covered by the chapters in this book, specific initiatives for the universities and their associations have been noted.

Advanced Graduate Training

Most of the recommendations in Chapter 2 are addressed to government and industry. Two areas of special responsibility to the universities themselves are the support of graduate student assistants and actions to maintain a vital faculty, which includes individuals of varied ages and experience.

□ Universities should continue to build into research budgets funds for the support of graduate student research assistants even when research funds are in short supply. The pressures of the moment should not be allowed to weaken the link between research and training that has made the American research university the enviably distinctive institution it is.

□ As economic conditions permit, universities should extend programs of voluntary early retirement for faculty in order to make room for the appointment of younger faculty.

□ Universities should develop on each campus programs and attitudes that encourage intellectual growth and change by faculty.

Industry-University Collaboration in Science

With the growing interest in agreements between research universities and industry, care must be taken to ensure that these agreements are to the advantage of both sides and that they do not threaten the traditional values of the university.

□ Universities must give careful thought to institutional policies with respect to such matters as patents and licenses and the handling of proprietary information and its implications for freedom of publication.

□ The Association of American Universities should take the lead in defining issues of common interest and in bringing together the appropriate people to articulate broadly applicable standards about these issues.

□ The universities need to become more sophisticated

in stimulating opportunities for collaboration with industry and in shaping them appropriately.

Research Libraries

As research libraries undergo a revolution in the ways they provide service to scholars, students, and other users, caused both by limited resources and by technological developments, the need for communication among scholars and librarians will increase, the role of the librarian will change, and the university will need to seek broad sources of funding.

☐ Universities should evaluate the effectiveness of communication and the involvement in policymaking on library issues of both faculty and library staff on their own campuses and should take whatever steps are needed to improve the processes.

☐ Universities should cooperate with research library groups and scholarly groups to establish a Research Library Council comprising scholars, research librarians, and research university administrators to promote the development of policies and guidelines in the areas of resource sharing, bibliographic standards and control, collection management and development, and preservation.

☐ The Association of American Universities and the Association of Research Libraries should establish a joint standing committee of research library directors, university presidents, and university chief academic officers to monitor needs and developments in library-scholarly communication and to develop new models of procedures to enhance such communication on individual campuses.

☐ The research universities and nonuniversity research library boards should establish a system of Centers of Special Responsibility through which responsibility for the acquisition, maintenance, and preservation of regional or national collections in particular topics or areas and responsibility for creating and maintaining the related data bases and for providing access to the collections might be divided among the libraries.

☐ Universities and their libraries should support the establishment of an initial phase of a national periodicals center by the Center for Research Libraries and the Association of Research Libraries and should work for the funding of a federally supported national periodicals system.

☐ Universities should give more information to business and industry about both the services and the problems of their research libraries and should increase the number of their requests to corporations for funds specifically to support library needs and special projects.

☐ Universities should reexamine and strengthen both the policy role and the salary structure and other rewards for research librarians and invest sufficient resources in professional library staffs to attract and keep people of the highest intellectual and managerial capacities.

Research Facilities and Instrumentation

The eroding physical base for research in universities has prompted a number of recommendations for action by government and industry to protect the ability of the universities to provide the research and training essential for economic health and national security. Universities must cooperate in the collection of the data needed for a full assessment of the deterioration in research facilities and instrumentation and must work to obtain federal, state, and private funding to meet the needs of their faculties and students in these areas.

International and Foreign Area Studies and Research

Universities need to work to convince both the federal government and industry of the value of international and area studies and research to foreign economic policy, national security, and the U.S. position in the world of international trade.

☐ Research universities should undertake, under the leadership of the Association of American Universities and the Social Science Research Council, to define the needs for research in the international field with a focus on knowledge of political, economic, and social processes embedded in the cultural contexts in which they exist in the real world.

☐ The universities need to come to terms with the federal government over the role of the Central Intelligence Agency in respect to universities and should explore ways to produce effective collaboration.

☐ Universities should establish cooperative ventures among Language and Area Studies Centers at several institutions in order to share resources, including regional library sharing programs for foreign studies.

☐ Universities should work with the National Council on Foreign Language and International Studies and firms or industry associations to plan and sponsor meetings between scholars and corporate leaders to identify ways in which international education and research at universities can help to meet the perceived needs of American business and industry.

INDEX

Designer: Marian O'Brien
Compositor: G & S Typesetters, Inc.
Printer: Vail-Ballou
Binder: Vail-Ballou
Text: Bembo
Display: Bembo

RICHARD G. COX LIBRARY
UN. OF SOUTHERN MISS. - GULF PARK